Hoof Beats From The Heart

Wes Kranz

iUniverse, Inc.
Bloomington

iUniverse books may be ordered through booksellers or by contacting:

iUniverse
1663 Liberty Drive
Bloomington, IN 47403
www.iuniverse.com
1-800-Authors (1-800-288-4677)

ISBN: 978-1-4502-8031-0 (sc)
ISBN: 978-1-4502-8032-7 (hc)
ISBN: 978-1-4502-8033-4 (ebook)

Printed in the United States of America

iUniverse rev. date: 12/30/2010

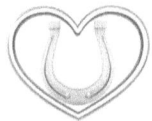

Stable of Contents

Acknowledgments   1

In Memory of Brie   3

Preface   5

Peanut's Plight   11

Woody's World   17

Maddie's Tail   25

Good Bye to Maddie   33

Dusty Toes   37

Brie's Bunch   41

Slice   49

Trigger   59

Peter and His Best Pal Patches   65

Reagan   69

Megan's Story   75

The Three Amigos   79

The Canadian Kids   83

Saying 'Goodbye' to an Old Friend   89

The 3 Cs & 3 Ts   93

Our Animal Assisted Therapy Activities   97

Happy Tails   101

Acknowledgments

We would like to thank our ferrier Sarah, for years of dedication to the "Thundering Herd." Your knowledge of horses reaches far beyond trimming hooves and Sue and I greatly appreciate the many insights you have shared with us over the years.

To Dr. Gary Batenhorst, DMV and Dr. Laura Orton, DMV, for sharing your irreplaceable knowledge, for taking the time to make an extra effort for the care of the animals, for always being there to answer our questions and for your compassion with the animals.

To Dr. Dan, "The Natural Horse Vet", DMV, for sharing your wealth of knowledge with us.

To the many volunteers that have assisted with the horses over the years. To Quinn, for your patience with Reagan. To Quinn's husband George for sharing his carpentry skills & for letting Quinn bring another man into her life. To Gina and Lucy, for helping replace our computer right in the middle of writing our stories. To Frank and Lynn, thank you for your enthusiasm to learn about horses. To Carissa for sharing your heart with Brie. To Amber, for overcoming your fear of horses and allowing them to share their gift of unconditional love with you.

To Nancy and Susan for your thoughtfulness is assisting with the care of our senior citizens. To Jim and Bonnie, for being there when we call. To Rich and Peggy, for 38 years of a special friendship. To Julie Otto, for sharing your wonderful talent as an artist drawing the illustrations. To Sharon and Jack, for your compassion for horses. To Heather and Teri, for photographing the thundering herd. To Charity, for sharing time from your hectic schedule to help us make this book a reality.

To Lois Last, Sue's mother and my mother-in law, thank you for all of your support throughout the years.

To Charles Wilhelm, international equine clinician, for being a friend and sharing your vast knowledge to help us better understand how to interact with our horses.

And finally to my wife Susan Marie. Your tremendous sacrifices and the tireless hours that you have given can never be appreciated enough in my heart. Mixing the special bowls of senior feed, tending to a scratch, holding them in your arms and kissing them goodbye when it is time to begin a new journey on the other side of the Rainbow Bridge, your gift of unconditional love for the animals is never ending. I know we sometimes wonder why we are doing this, but one look in their eyes and our question is answered. Thank you for being my best friend, my soul mate and my loving wife.

In Memory of Brie

"And God took a handful of southerly wind,
blew his breath over it and created the horse."
-Bedouin Myth-

To Brie and those before her who have made the journey....
Thank you for sharing your gift of unconditional love....

Your soft nickers and gentle nudges will be missed....
But always remembered in our hearts....

Brie

Preface

Born in 1954 in Oshkosh, Wisconsin, I grew up on a city street that lead to a horse farm a couple of miles out of town. Back in those days when the north end of Spruce Street reached Murdock Avenue, that was basically the end of the city limits and once you crossed Murdock Avenue you were on Vinland Road. There were a few houses located near the intersection on Vinland Road and after that it was basically farmland and woods. But if you followed the gravel road a little farther you would see a white board fence surrounding a horse farm called Turner Farm. They raised and trained trotting horses and also boarded horses. If my mother said it was ok, I'd get on my trusty Schwinn bicycle and head out on the fifteen minute ride to see the horses. I would lay my bike down in the ditch along the road and head up to the fence to see if there were any horses in the pastures. The farm had four or five different pastures surrounding an oval horse track that was used for training. I would always try to sneak some apples or carrots out of the house to feed the horses. I can remember my mother once asking me if I had forgotten something as I was about to leave, so I'm guessing she could tell when a few apples or carrots were missing. The horses weren't really friendly, but every once in awhile I could get a horse to walk near the fence and I would toss a carrot or apple to them. It was a bonus day if I could get them to take one out of my hand and rub their head for a few seconds. Sometimes I would forget how long I had been there and my dad would drive out and tell me it was time to come home.

In one of the city parks, someone offered pony rides during the summer months and I could name every horse they used in their pony ring. Thirty five years later, when we were looking for a pony ring to purchase, as fate would have it we bought the same pony ring that I had ridden around so many times in the late fifties and early sixties. My mother would take me down to the park so I could go for a pony ride and when I was old enough I would ride my bike down to the park whenever I could to see the ponies.

All my scrapbooks growing up are filled with any thing relating to horses. Photos, pictures torn out of a magazine, pages from a calendar…if it had something to do with horses, it was in one of the scrapbooks my mother had made for me. Then there was the horse collection that I accumulated during my childhood years - over 300 model horses that I collected. Whenever we took a family vacation I could get a model horse from the different places and states we visited and sometimes Santa would bring me a model horse at Christmas.

My parents often played cards with some friends that they had known for years a couple of times a month and they raised trotting horses. It was about a forty five minute drive to their farm and if I had done all my chores I was assigned to do around the house we would leave early Saturday morning to visit them. If I didn't have my chores done by Saturday, we wouldn't leave until they were finished. It didn't take long for me to realize I needed to cut the lawn after school on Thursdays or Fridays.

When we got to their farm, the first thing I would do after jumping out of the back seat of the car was call out their dog's name and head for the pasture to see the horses. "Mugs" was a boxer and as soon as she saw me she would race over to meet me and nearly knock me down on the ground. I'm sure there were a few times that she did. I wasn't allowed to go in the pastures because one of the horses would chase you, but I could climb on the fence boards to pet them and feed them apples. When Herbbie went down to the barn to feed the horses or fill their water tanks, I could go along and help him. Sometimes he would even let me clip the chain attached to their feed box in the box stalls to their halters while they ate their grain and he would also let me help feed the hay to each one of them.

My eyes would swell up to the point of nearly being shut when I was around the horses all day and I would have to put a cold damp washcloth over them. My mother took me to the family doctor and we discovered I had allergies and may be allergic to horses, hay or something else around a farm. The doctor gave my mother a prescription for some little blue pills. I can remember taking one the night before we were going to Herbbie and Bertha's and then one pill when we arrived and one at the end of the day. I don't know what those little blue pills were, but they sure did work and after a couple of years I outgrew the allergy.

I'm sure I drove Herbbie nuts whenever we went to visit them. I was always asking if it was time to feed the horses or get them in from the outer pastures into the barnyard. Then one Saturday when we pulled into their driveway Bertha said I needed to go down to the barn right away. I ran down into the barn and Herbbie was feeding the horses so I asked if he needed any help. He said they were all fed except the one in the end box stall. I grabbed a flake of hay and headed towards the box stall, but I couldn't see a horse in the stall as I approached it. I looked in the box stall and there stood a small brown dappled pony with a whitish mane and tail. Ginger was a Shetland pony about 40 inches tall at her shoulders. Herbbie had bought Ginger from the mink farm that was located on the other side of the fence line along one of the pastures. The mink farm raised hundreds of mink and Herbbie said they would buy unwanted horses and slaughter them to feed the mink. I didn't know if that was true or not, but I was sure glad he bought Ginger for ten dollars from them. There was an old bridle hanging next to Ginger's box stall and Herbbie said if I could figure out how to put it on her, he would let me ride her in the pasture. I had seen the ponies at the park with bridles on, saw all kinds of photos with horses and bridles and I watched Matt Dillon on *Gunsmoke* ride his horse every Saturday night, so how hard could it be to figure out? I knew how to put a halter on a horse and figured out that it kind of went on the same way, but I couldn't figure out how the bit went in her mouth. I would get it in Ginger's mouth, but not over her tongue. After several attempts Herbbie showed me how to do it and then all I needed was a saddle. Ginger couldn't be ridden with a saddle. Whenever she was saddled she would buck like a rodeo horse, but you could ride her bareback.

The thought of the fact that the only horses I had ever ridden on where the ponies at the park never crossed my mind. We walked Ginger out into the barnyard and I managed to pull myself up on to her back. We just stood there and Ginger wouldn't move an inch. I slapped her on the butt, kicked with my legs, tugged with the reins and we just stood there. Herbbie stood nearby laughing at me. He told me to grab some of her mane and then make a kissing sound as I tapped her sides with my legs. It worked and we were moving. I would ride Ginger whenever Herbbie said I could, but I would have to catch her in the pasture and put her bridle on myself.

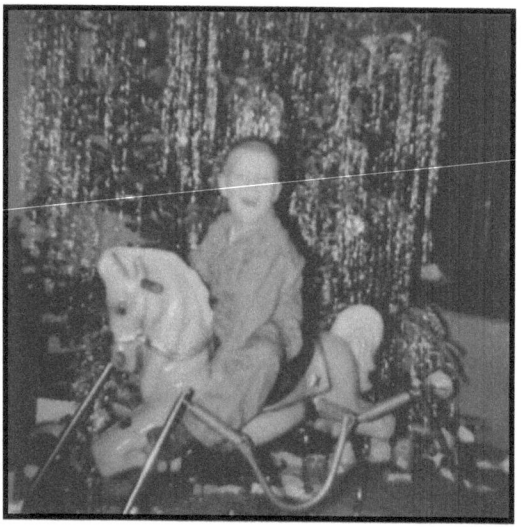

Wes spending time on the Ranch

Now there is something you should know about Ginger. She was a fun little pony to ride, but she had a couple of slightly bad habits. She would run like the wind and suddenly drop down on her front knees as if she was sliding into second base. Upon doing this, I usually exited her rather quickly right over the top of her neck and head. As I would roll on the ground, Ginger would quickly turn and head up the large hill in the pasture stopping at the top to eat grass. It always seemed like a long way back to the top of that hill to get Ginger. One day after Ginger had dropped to her knees and I went flying, I walked all the way up that hill to get back on her and she wouldn't move. I even got off her and tried to drag her down the hill. My parents and Herbbie and Bertha were playing cards on their porch and he yelled out "get a little stick and tap her on the butt." I found a small stick, climbed back on Ginger and tapped her a few times. After several attempts without moving I threw the stick down and without any warning we were off to the races. I forgot to mention something else. At the bottom of the hill there was a water tank against the fence and on the other side of the fence was the outhouse. Now we had ridden down this hill many a time and Ginger always turned at the last second and we would narrowly miss hitting the side of the water tank with my leg, so I wasn't to concerned that we were heading in that direction again. But even as a ten or eleven year old child there comes a time when you realize you're going awful fast and the fence is getting awful close. Suddenly Ginger dropped to her knees and away I went! Over the water tank and fence and heading straight for the back of the outhouse. As I remember, there was a crash, probably the sound of breaking boards and then the thud of a child rolling on the ground after he flew through the open door of the outhouse. As I lay on the ground wondering what happened I heard a voice say, "Go get back up on that pony. You never end on a bad day." By this time Ginger was back at the top of the hill eating grass waiting for me. Half crawling back up the hill, I got back on Ginger and we walked down the hill and back into the barnyard like nothing ever happened. I gave her a handful of sugar cubes after I took her bridle off and she nudged my arm for some more.

A few years later, Herbbie and Bertha sold their farm to a housing developer and bought a farm near Oshkosh. The first time we visited their new farm, I ran out to the barn to see the horses. But they were all gone, including Ginger. I never asked what happened to the horses. I couldn't understand why the horses were gone. Several months later, my parents told me the horses were sold because Herbbie was ill and had cancer. Now in my early teens, it seemed like horses were out of my life.

While attending the University of Wisconsin Platteville, I worked for the horticulture department which had a large garden trial plot and orchard located on the university's college farm. Occasionally I'd help doing some of the general farm daily activities, helping in the swine unit, dairy unit or general farm chores. The farm had a few horses for a horse production class they offered and every chance I had, a friend and I would venture down to the barn they were kept in to spend some time hanging out with the horses. Rumor had it, unless you were or had taken the horse production class the professor didn't want anyone to associate with the horses. Maybe that's why they seemed so timid. And as they say, things happen and maybe someone would sneak a few apples to the horses and maybe even sat on them bareback.

The years went by and in 1984 Sue and I were married. Ten years later we were living in the country offering educational programs at the ranch. It was during the summer of 1994 that Peanut arrived at the ranch and Sue and I realized we needed to open our hearts to horses in need of a second chance in their lives.

Peanut's Plight

Peanut was twenty five years old when he arrived at the ranch. He was a Buckskin with a glossy black mane and tail and was around 14 hands tall. We received a phone call from someone that lived in a town about 10 miles from us asking if we would be interested in a gentle horse that anyone could ride and wasn't bothered by anything. The individual really didn't want to deal with a horse anymore and said we could have him for four hundred dollars. I explained that we really weren't interested, but we would go and take a look at the horse in case we ran across someone looking for a gentle horse.

We were told we could go look at the horse anytime we wanted to, because Peanut was always in the pasture. I was familiar with the area, so the directions we were given were easy to follow. When we turned down the dirt lane and followed it until it stopped by a pasture gate, we were shocked by what we saw - A horse with a twenty foot heavy rope tied to his halter and the other end of the rope tied to an old rusty car in an open field. There was a five gallon pail tipped over that was used for water. The grassy area had been worn down to nothing but dirt in a hundred and eighty degree semi circle from pacing back and forth around the car. The only shade available was from a large oak tree for a couple of hours a day when the sun passed by it. Peanut was pacing back and forth pulling at the rope as we approached him. He was very anxious, perhaps thinking we had brought him more water or some hay to eat. We untied the rope from the car bumper and walked Peanut over to another area in the field where he could munch on some grass. We picked his feet up to see what his reaction would be to a ferrier and Peanut stood perfectly still munching grass as we lifted each leg and held his hoof for a few moments. It was mid-June and Peanut appeared to be in fairly good condition. He was also slightly sway backed and had a parrot bite when we examined his teeth.

We knew as soon as we saw Peanut tied to the car bumper that he was going to be coming home with us, so we drove into town to stop by the owner's home. I knocked on the door and spoke with a woman about Peanut coming home with us. She said we could pick him up after she rode in an area parade that was coming up and he would be back at the pasture were we had just come from. A few weeks after the parade, we received a call from the woman saying we could go pick up Peanut and we could swing by her house to pay for him on the way back through town. It had been about a month since we first saw Peanut and as we drove up to the gate we could see his summer coat was a light brown color contrasted by his black mane and tail. After we turned the trailer around and open the door, we untied Peanut from the bumper and promised him he would never be tied again. Sue had cut several apples into slices in case we needed a treat to help get him into the trailer. After eating a few apples slices we walked near the trailer and Peanut didn't seemed to be bothered by it and we walked right into it. I gave him a couple more apple slices after tying the lead rope for the trip home. On our way back to the ranch, we stopped by the woman's house to pay her for Peanut. She met me at the door and said thank you and then mentioned that Peanut had an issue with fences and that was why he was tied to the car bumper.

Upon arriving back at the ranch, we unloaded Peanut and walked him around the outside fencing so he could take in his new surroundings. A couple of the horses walked up to the gate and we let them greet each other and no one seemed to care about a new arrival. After meeting a few more of the horses, we put Peanut into an outer pasture area where he could spend the next few days getting used to his new surroundings. Later in the afternoon we heard a squeaky noise coming from where Peanut was. As we walked towards the pasture we could see that he was leaning against the two by six boards that made up the top railing of the fence. He was standing by the wooden post that held the boards up and was pushing on them with his chest and neck. He would rock back and forth against the boards. We went into the pasture with him and he calmed right down and he started to meander around munching on the grass. About an hour later we heard the same noise again and sure enough Peanut was pushing on the boards and this time had succeeded in pushing the top board from the post. I reattached the two by six boards and as we away he started pushing against the fence again. Within thirty minutes he had managed to push all four boards off the post so he could walk out of the pasture. I put the boards back in place using some larger nails and returned Peanut to the pasture. Peanut walked over to another area of the pasture and started pushing on a different post trying to loosen the boards. So we decided to put him in a box stall for the night. When I checked on him during the night, he was trying to figure out how he could chew his way through the box stall. In the morning you could see where Peanut must have been crossed with a beaver. He had chewed two of the two by six boards that made up the lower portion of the box stall nearly in half and had tried chewing about a dozen other boards. For the next couple of days Peanut would walk up and down the pasture fence testing just about every post pushing against the boards with his chest. After sitting in a chair watching him walk around for a couple of hours, I had one of those "light bulb" moments where something clicks in your mind. Just open the gate and let the goofy horse walk around the ranch by himself. I took off his halter and said "there you go" and he just started walking around the ranch like he had been there forever. There was a stock tank near the barn gate and he quickly learned that when he wanted a drink he'd just walk up from the outer area of the ranch to get a drink. Peanut never bothered the outside fencing around the ranch and as long as he could walk around at his leisure he was content. One day I was going to do some work in the garden and decided to take Peanut along so he could eat some of the grass nearby. A attached a twenty foot lead rope to his halter so if he walked away too far I could grab the lead rope and pull him closer to me. As time went by Peanut slowly would walk twenty or thirty yards from me and I would ask him where he thought he was going. He'd slowly lift up his head from grazing and walk towards me, and then he would turn around and slowly head back in the opposite direction. I'd go and pick up the lead rope and bring him back to the gate of our inner fenced in area. After a few days I noticed that Peanut didn't like the traffic that went by the ranch. When a car would approach, he'd turn and walk away from it heading towards the pasture area. One day I had forgotten to close our outside gate and noticed Peanut wasn't around. I looked out by the garden area and noticed Peanut was walking along the outer fence line eating the grass. I went to get a halter and lead rope and when I reached the gate called out his name. Peanut lifted up hid head and slowly walked all the way around the outer fence and came in right through the gate walking up to me. I rubbed his neck and told him he was a good boy for coming to me when I called him. From that day on whenever I was doing something outside, Peanut was allowed to go off and munch some grass between our outer fencing and the neighbor's driveway that ran along the backside of our property. For the next eight years, Peanut would enjoy going out for his walks. I'd leave the gate open for him and when he wanted a drink he'd come up to get one and then off he'd go to munch on some grass again.

Peanut was a very good horse. He loved to go trail riding and ride in parades. Children as young as seven years old would take him out for a ride and he was a perfect gentleman. When the older volunteers or I would get on him to go for a ride in the winter, he really wanted to play games. We had used Peanut to help teach some of the other horses how to trail ride by having them walk with him wherever we went. Peanut would walk up or down a slope, through water or snow and the other horses would learn by following him.

There was a grove of evergreen trees near one of the trails we would ride and Peanut would love to try and rub you out of the saddle by walking through the branches. If you didn't hang on to the saddle horn, he would darn near push you right out of the saddle. When Peanut would trot or canter, he would always drift off to his left and whenever he had the chance during the winter months and we rode near that group of evergreens, you'd find yourself full of needles.

A year after Peanut arrived, we received a phone call from someone that wanted to find a home for a pony that their child had outgrown. The pony was walking around with the dairy cows and they really wanted to find someone to take him. It was about 15 miles to their farm so I thought I'd bring the trailer along just in case Rusty was going to come home with me. I drove down the long driveway to the farm and saw a small pony tied to an oak tree. Rusty was about forty inches tall and a bay color with a golden brown mane and tail. He was a very sweet little guy badly in need of a hoof trimming. His front hooves looked like a pair of clown shoes and he had floundered. I met the parents and the husband explained that their children had outgrown Rusty and they just wanted to give him to a good home. Rusty jumped right into the trailer and we headed home to meet someone that was waiting for him. When we arrived at the ranch, Rusty was nickering back and forth to another horse before we could even get him out of the trailer. Peanut had run over to the gate and he was all excited to meet the new arrival. We put a lead rope on Peanut and let him meet Rusty and they became instant best buddies. For the next seven years, Rusty and Peanut were inseparable, never walking anywhere around the ranch without each other. They would eat and sleep together and Peanut would teach Rusty to munch on the grass along the outside of the fence when we would let them out together. Watching them together, you would have thought they had been pasture buddies for years. Within two days Peanut had shown Rusty where the water was by the barn gate and how to walk in and out of the gate to go eat grass.

Peanut was always walking around the ranch somewhere and when we would call his name he'd meander up to us looking for a treat. One morning we noticed he wasn't around and we called his name. We didn't hear his deep whinny sound he would make when we called his name. We walked over to the backside of the barn and Peanut was lying down with his head up and his eyes were glossy. It was Peanut's time to make the journey across the Rainbow Bridge. I called the clinic explaining we needed someone to stop by to put Peanut to sleep. Someone was in the area and as soon as they were finished with that call they would be right over. When the vet arrived we walked over to Peanut and she held her stethoscope to his heart and said his heart valves weren't closing and he was basically having a heart attack. As we held Peanut's head in our arms, Peanut was given an injection and he fell asleep.

We always joked that Peanut had two speeds, fast and faster. As soon as you finished saddling him, he was ready to go. You would no more than get settled in the saddle and Peanut would try to start walking at a brisk pace and sneak into a trot if you would let him. A few steps later he was ready to canter or break into a gallop and Peanut loved to gallop. After a fresh snowfall Peanut couldn't wait to go for a ride. He'd run through the snow with clumps of snow flying off his hooves and if you were riding behind him it was like you were trying to dodge snowballs from a snowball fight. When we would finish riding and he was unsaddled, Peanut would drop his head to the ground and fall over on his side rolling back and forth from one side completely flipping him over to the other side. He would get up making a big sigh and then shake all the snow off.

And that's how we will remember Peanut, running through a fresh snowfall with snow flying off his hooves as he heads for those evergreens.

Woody's World

Woody arrived at the ranch Memorial Day weekend in 1998 and for the next ten years we would learn how a blind horse adapted to his surroundings and led a normal life. I had been reading the horses for sale section of an area agriculture paper and I noticed an ad for a 20 year old blind Appaloosa. The ad stated the owners were asking six hundred dollars. The horse had stood for the ferrier, had been trailered, trail ridden and had been updated on his vaccinations. I decided to call the number and see if I could get some additional information about Woody. A woman answered the phone and as we talked seemed to be relieved that I had called. She told me they had purchased Woody from someone in Iowa and that he had been partially blind nearly his entire life. Apparently when Woody was around two years old he drank some contaminated ground water and had developed leptospirosis, a disease horses can get from drinking water that has been contaminated by deer. She explained they had owned Woody for several years and he was a great trail riding horse and anyone could ride him. The reason they had decided to sell Woody was because some of the other horses had started to chase him around the pasture and barnyard. Recently a horse had chased him through a fence and he nearly ran over the edge of a large area where they were digging a pond. On another occasion a horse cornered Woody in the barnyard and kicked him several times opening large gashes on his hind legs that required stitches.

The Memorial Day weekend was coming up and I said I could drive up to see Woody on Sunday. In the meantime I searched for information about leptospirosis and also called our vet to see if they could tell me any additional information about the disease.

Woody

Since it was about a three hour drive one way to where Woody was in North Central Wisconsin, I decided to take the trailer along having already decided he would come home with me if everything worked out. As I pulled into the driveway I noticed several horses in a pasture and there was a large Appaloosa near a gate. The woman I had spoken with on the phone greeted me at the porch door and we walked out to see Woody. On the way to the pasture she mentioned they had someone pull into their driveway a few days earlier and the individual had offered them sixty cents a pound for Woody. A horse jockey was going through the area buying horses for slaughter and he had also seen their ad in the paper. When we reached the gate, the woman called Woody's name and he turned his head as she opened the gate. Woody was a big guy and I was guessing he had to be over 17 hands tall and he was an Appaloosa/Standard bred cross. As we walked Woody out of the pasture the first thing I noticed were two large gashes on his hind legs, one in the shape of a large "U" was about six inches long. Woody had been pinned against the barn by another horse and kicked again. I walked Woody around their yard with a lead rope and he seemed a little leery of his surroundings, slowly snorting puffs of air out his nostrils as he sniffed the grass. After a few minutes he decided it was ok and starting eating some grass as we continued to talk about the big guy. I saddled and bridled Woody and rode him up and down the driveway a few times and could see he loved to go for rides and that he also had learned to neck rein. With the gentle touch of the reins against his neck, Woody would turn left or right and would come to a stop just by asking him to with little rein pressure. After unsaddling him I gave Woody an apple, which disappeared in two bites and he was nudging his forehead against me looking for more treats. I lifted each foot to see how he reacted for a ferrier and he stood like a statue.

After spending just a few minutes with Woody, I was glad I decided to bring the trailer with me and knew he would be coming home. The family had decided they wanted to donate Woody to us for use in our animal assisted therapy programs. And over the next ten years, Woody's story would be shared with thousands of children and adults. I opened the trailer door and as Woody approached the trailer I asked him to step up and noticed he took two large steps, which reminded me of the children's game "Simon Says". When Simon said take two large steps, everyone tried to take the longest steps they could reaching out as far as one could with their leg. Woody reached out with one leg as if to be feeling for the floor of the trailer and when he put his first leg in the trailer, he reached in with his other leg and then just walked right in the trailer. I tied him to the trailer and slowly closed the door behind him and he settled right in ready for the journey home. Everyone rubbed his nose as they said good bye to Woody and we started the trip home. I stopped about every hour to check on how he was riding and he was doing really well. Occasionally I could feel him shifting his weight around in the trailer, but other than that he trailered like he did it every day.

Upon arriving back at the ranch, some of the horses came up to the fence along the driveway to investigate the new arrival. As I unloaded Woody, a few neighs and slight snorts were exchanged and I let a couple of the horses walk up to greet him over the fence and smell each others noses. We knew Woody was completely blind in his left eye and the eye lid was closed. Woody had some sight in his right eye, but how much was very hard to determine. His eye was very clouded from the disease he had lived with throughout the years. Sue and I led him around the pasture he would have access to and let him explore the boundaries He could sense the electric tape fence we had and would actually come to a stop a few feet from it. The electric tape was about two inches wide and moved just slightly and Woody could detect the movement of the electric tape. We walked him through the barn to his box stall where he would spend the next few days getting use to his new surrounding and sounds. For the next few days we would feed Woody in his stall and then take him for walks out to the pasture and slowly introduce him to the other horses. We put a 20 foot lead rope on his halter so he could explore where things were and if we needed could pull him back. Watching Woody, we quickly realized how Woody's world must have appeared to him. He could walk through the open door of the barn to go out to the pasture after he'd stop for a few seconds before he walked through it. As he approached a wooden fence made from 2 by 6's he'd suddenly stop to approach it, smell it and then touch it with his nose. We also noticed that he could not see a fence made with cattle panels and he'd walk into them. At the time, a portion of our pasture was divided into sections using 16 foot long cattle panels. So we removed all the fencing we had dividing our pastures and opened everything up so Woody could move around with out the worry of running into a fence. He couldn't see the wire panels, but he could see the shape of the 2x6's used for our perimeter fence around the ranch.

Woody's world of sight was a world of different shades of black and gray. The barn wall may have appeared dark to him and the door opening a lighter shade and he learned that the lighter shaded area was the door opening. We always put a fly mask over Woody's eyes to protect them from the direct sunlight during the summer months and during the winter to help reduce the sun's reflection off the snow. If the day was slightly overcast or cloudy, Woody could easily make his way around the ranch without the fly mask. Whenever we would go riding with him, we always took a fly mask along to protect his eyes. We quickly noticed that when Woody would go for a ride down the road, he could not detect what the white line was that ran along the shoulder of the road. As he approached it he would make a slight snort lowering his head down towards it and turn sideways trying to avoid walking on it. He did the same thing with the center line down the middle of the road. Woody wouldn't step over it and would almost walk sideways trying to determine what the line was. One would guess his depth perception was almost non existent, so he couldn't determine if he should step up over the line or step down going over the line. When a horse approaches a stream and we ask them to cross it, they naturally put their head down to sniff the water and look at it. They have no way of telling if the water is two inches deep or two feet deep. To help Woody overcome his fear of the lines, we walked with him and using the lead rope to guide him across the lines. After stopping several times to explore the lines, Woody eventually learned to walk across the lines without coming to a complete stop. He would lower his head when he approached the lines and step right across them. On a sunny day Woody would also have problems with the shadow from trees going across the road and we just repeated the process of walking him across the shadows until he felt comfortable.

Whenever we approached an area that would require Woody to go up an incline or down a slope we asked Woody to "step up" or "step down" and that would become his cue to walk safely wherever we went.

Three weeks after Woody arrived at the ranch we were participating in Wisconsin's celebration of its 150th anniversary of becoming a state. Two wagon trains were going to travel across parts of Wisconsin recreating a portion of the frontier routes traveled by settlers as they past through Wisconsin. One of the wagon trains was going to passing about thirty miles from us, so we had decided to participate in it for a couple of days. We'd travel about twenty two miles a day with the wagon train, I was an out rider riding along with the covered wagons and Sue walked along side the wagons with several individuals as walkers.

To prepare for the wagon train, we walked about ten to twelve miles every other day for the three weeks leading up to our joining the train. I would take Woody out for rides every other day gradually increasing the distances from a couple of miles to ten miles. Our vet had examined Woody a few days after he arrived and after examining him, it was thought he was probably thirty years old instead of twenty years old. His teeth were showing signs of a much older horse, which I had suspected when I had originally look at his bite. Otherwise he was in great health and the vet said he should be fine participating in the wagon train. Sarah, our ferrier had put front shoes on Woody two weeks before the wagon train so he would have a chance to get used to them. The previous owners had also had shoes put on Woody, so he was used to wearing them. Sarah checked the shoes a couple of days before we left to join the wagon train and everything was fine.

Woody was a real trooper in the 1998 wagon train. We would travel about twenty two miles the first day we participated and 18 miles the second day. All the practicing we had done getting him used to shadows from trees, the white line along the side of a road and the center lines really helped make it a great experience. And Woody would teach us another lesson in how a blind horse could lead a normal life. We knew someone that was also riding in the wagon train and had asked them if we could ride along with them, explaining it would be good idea for Woody to walk with another horse. As we started riding I noticed Woody quickly started walking on the left side of the horse next to the horse's hindquarters. Woody still had some degree of sight in his left eye, so this only made sense that he could see the horse he was walking with. Then we noticed something else. Every few minutes Woody would reach out with his nose and gently touch the hindquarter of the horse gauging his distance from the horse until he became comfortable walking next to it.

In the many rides to come with Woody, he would learn to bump the hindquarters of the horse he would be riding next to and then put his head and neck on the rider's leg and begin rubbing it with his head. This would become a game with Woody and he would rub so hard with his head he could push the person right up in the saddle. Woody would participate in the 1999 and 2000 wagon train reunions, as well as many parades during the next ten years.

A month after Woody came to the ranch another horse arrived and the two would become best friends. Woody walked around the pastures without any real problems and mixed into the group of horses he was with, but didn't really seem to pal up with any one horse in particular. This changed almost instantly when a quarter horse named Maddie arrived. We were looking for another horse for our equine therapy activities when we heard there was a "bomb proof" horse going to a sale and most likely would be sold for slaughter. Upon arriving at the ranch, Maddie and Woody greeted each other and within minutes were rubbing their necks on each other and started grooming each other. For whatever reason, they instantly became best friends and would walk together around the ranch for the next ten years.

Maddie would become Woody's eyes and would be at his side leading him around the ranch, walking with him on trail rides or next to him in parades. Maddie would let Woody smell where she was and rub on her hindquarter as they walked together. If Maddie would get too far ahead of Woody, he would make a soft nicker to her and she would slow down or actually stop and wait for him to come up to her until he could touch her hindquarter with his nose. Then they would start walking again. As I mentioned earlier, Woody loved to walk along side of Maddie and start rubbing his head on her left side. Many a volunteer had Woody put his head behind their knees while their foot was in the stirrup nearly lifting them right up in the saddle. If you tried to push his head away, he would place his head on your leg until you rubbed between his ears.

When we would have school groups or organizations visit the ranch for a tour, Woody would be right there to greet them with Maddie, and everyone would ask how a blind horse could walk around the ranch. We would ask everyone to close their eyes and pretend if you were a blind horse how would you walk around the ranch and of the five senses a person has what ones would you use to communicate. After a few seconds we would get a few guesses. You could smell, touch and use your ears to communicate with another horse. One of the first things horses do when they meet each other for the first time is to smell each other's noses and exchange a puff of air from their nose.

Throughout the day our horses greet each other by touching noses. By listening with his ears, Woody usually had a good idea where Maddie was and if needed, he would whinny to get her attention or Maddie would give a soft whinny to let Woody know she was nearby. Woody's ability to use his sense of touch to communicate with Maddie was truly a special bond between two animals. Wherever they would go, Woody would always bump her hind quarters to keep in contact with her. Walking in the pastures, trail riding or participating in parades, Woody would be right next to Maddie bumping her to keep in contact. This may not seem like a big deal to anyone, but when trotting or cantering it was amazing how Woody could lope right along never hesitating because of his lack of sight.

On a Monday morning around 6 a.m., Woody had laid down and died in his sleep with Maddie standing by his side. Sue called me at work saying Woody had just died and I said I'd be there in twenty minutes. When I arrived home, I rushed into the barn and Woody was laying on his side with Maddie right next to him as if to be keeping watch over him.

We called our vet and Dr. Laura arrived within an hour. At the age of 40 years old, Woody's heart had told him it was time to cross the Rainbow Bridge.

Maddie's Tail

In the summer of 1998, we would bring home one of the best horses we have ever had at the ranch in 16 years. And it all started with a simple phone call. In 1997, we started an animal assisted therapy program for children with special needs in elementary schools in an area school system. It was very rewarding and the children really benefited from the program. During our first pilot program we realized that some of the students had outgrown our ponies and we decided to look for a horse that everyone could ride. We had purchased some of our tack equipment from an individual who also bought and sold horses so I thought I'd give him a call to see if he could help us locate a horse for our programs. As it turned out he was supposed to pick up a horse within the next few days from someone in the area and take it to a sale barn and he thought it might be worth a trip to go look at it. He gave us their phone number, I gave them a call and as they say "the rest is history".

It would take me about an hour to drive down to see what would turn out to be a very special horse. A veterinarian owned the horse, so I made arrangements to stop by their veterinary clinic to meet him. His wife greeted me inside their office and said her husband was still with a client and that I could drive out to their farm to take a look at the horse. She would be in a pasture with several other horses and I could run her into the barn yard and her saddle and bridle were in the tack room. On the way back through town I could stop back in and let me know what I decided. They were asking $800 for the horse.

I drove out to their farm and as I pulled up to the barn noticed several horses grazing in a small pasture that was connected to a barn yard area. I found a halter and lead rope and grabbed a few horse treats from a bag and headed out towards the pasture. I was warned that the horse might be a little hard to catch and I soon began calling a name that Sue and I would call thousands of times over the next nine years. "Maddie? Come on Maddie!" A small Quarter horse lifted her head and started heading for the opposite end of the pasture. I had left the barnyard gate open thinking everyone would head in that direction once I had them turned around. Well even the best ideas sometime don't work out and Maddie and the other horses ran right by the gate and just running circles around me. Realizing the horses were having the last laugh, I went into the barn and grabbed a bale of hay. After I put the bale in the feed bunk in the barn yard the horses walked in for a bite to eat.

That is all but one...Maddie. She still wanted to walk around the pasture a few more times and then she just stopped in her tracks waiting for me to walk over and put her halter on.

Maddie

Now that I had my forty five minute workout in, I walked Maddie over to a hitching post to put her saddle on. Once saddled, Maddie was a very easy horse to ride responding to everything I asked her to do. After taking her saddle off, I picked up each foot and crawled underneath her from her left and right side. I waved the blanket around her head and tossed it on her back from a few feet away to see if she had any reaction. She just stood there never moving an inch. I put Maddie back into the pasture and stopped by the clinic to let them know we would take her. We made plans to pick her up the next day. Returning the next day I stopped by the clinic again and the receptionist said they would meet me at their farm and I should go ahead and pick Maddie up. I drove out to their farm and this time Maddie was in the small barn yard waiting for me. As I opened the trailer door Maddie was right there to walk into the trailer. No one seemed to be coming so I decided to head back to the clinic and about half way back I saw a veterinary pickup truck heading towards me. I pulled over to the side of the road and we exchanged introductions and talked for a few minutes about Maddie. He gave me her vaccination papers, I gave him a check and Maddie was on her way to a new home.

Maddie was a very quiet horse and fit in with the other horses at the ranch without any problems. She was about 15 hands high and had a unique color to her coat. She had kind of a light reddish brown color and we've really never seen another Quarter horse with that color since; then again Maddie would always prove to be a little different. When I brought her home the first thing Sue noticed was that Maddie had rubbed her tail off right up to her tail bone. The vet had mentioned that she did like boys and had been a brood mare having her last foal when she was right around the age of fifteen. And we soon noticed that when she came into heat she would walk up to the fence by the other horses and rub her tail against it. She would continuously do this and actually rub the skin off the tip of her tail bone. We had Dr. Laura stop to take a look at her and jokingly decided she just liked boys. After a couple of years she finally seemed to outgrow rubbing her tail against the fence, but she still liked to tease boys.

In the fall of 1998, we would take Maddie to meet the school children in our animal assisted therapy programs. She was an instant hit with the children and would be for the next several years. She would literally get mugged by the children and she would just stand there and fall asleep. Children could be crawling underneath her, sitting in the saddle and brushing her all at once and she could fall asleep or do a darn good job of pretending to be sleeping. Maddie loved to go for walks with the children at the schools. We would put a twenty foot lead rope on her halter and all the children would grab the rope and off we'd go. A few children in the special needs classes were confined to a wheel chair. So while they held on to Maddie's lead rope I would walk behind them pushing their wheel chair. At one school that was two blocks from a fast food restaurant we would do something special for the last visit of the school year. We would have a wagon train carrying the children through the drive thru window so they could order ice cream. Maddie, Brie, Dusty and Bonnie would be the saddle horses and Strawberry would pull a pony cart. Five horses with twelve children riding down the sidewalk was an unusual site and many a person going by in their cars had to look twice.

Maddie also visited nursing homes and senior citizen centers throughout Northeastern Wisconsin. We were visiting a nursing home and one of the nurses asked us if they could borrow her for a few minutes. Before we knew it Maddie was gone and we could see her walking down the hallways visiting patients in their rooms. At another nursing home, a ninety two year young individual asked if he could go for a ride on Maddie. We were given permission to let him sit in the saddle and with little assistance he climbed right up into the saddle and then he asked to go for a ride around the parking lot. When he climbed down out of the saddle he told stories of his family using horses on their farm and how he use to ride a pony to school. He had horses of his own until he was in his late seventies.

I had been teaching Maddie to respond to hand and voice signals and she was a quick learner. While asking her to walk forward or stop I would either lower or raise my hands for the appropriate request. Eventually I could just use my hands to signal Maddie asking her to walk stop or turn and she also learned to stand and stay until I would ask her to walk toward me.

One summer an area restaurant that had a western theme asked us to give horse rides and let their customers have their picture taken with them for a few hours each Saturday afternoon. After the customers finished eating they would come out to meet the horses. Maddie would usually close her eyes and just doze off between visits with children and they would get a big smile when I asked her to wake up. I'd give her a hand signal and she would follow me around the parking lot. One afternoon after a couple of cars had pulled out of two parking stalls right next to each other we walked Maddie into one of them and I asked her to stand and stay. I walked about fifteen feet over to the sidewalk and then signaled her to walk over to me and she meandered over in her usual slow stride. We put her back in the parking stall asking her to stand and stay again. Cars would pull into the parking lot and they would get out of their car and see Maddie with her eyes closed and her head lowered. People would walk over to her and she would open her eyes and never move an inch.

When school groups visited the ranch, Maddie would meander over to the children to get some attention and that was always a good opportunity to ask them if they had ever seen a battery operated horse. After saddling Maddie I would show the children a small battery and explain that Maddie needed two batteries to make her move. Placing my hand under the saddle I'd pull out another battery. And of course during this time Maddie would be day dreaming and she had no intention of moving so I could pat her on the neck, tug on her tail and ever wiggle her lips. So then I'd put the batteries back under her saddle and cue her to pretend wake up and take a few steps. Some of the kindergarten and first grade children would just be amazed and I would tell the adults that the local farm supply store would have the battery operated horses in aisle 21. I remember running into a parent that had been a chaperone on his daughters field trip to the ranch and he said his daughter insisted that they go look for that battery operated horse. Maddie also loved to show the children how we pulled loose teeth in a horse's mouth. She would shake her head up and down when I asked her if she had a loose tooth. Pretending to the tooth, I'd slide small pliers near her mouth and put an old tooth in it. The kids would help me count to three and then giving Maddie a cue she would pull her head back and out would come the tooth. So we would have to talk to the kids about how important it was to brush their teeth every day.

Maddie would go for walks with Peanut and Dusty along the fence line to munch on grass during the day when we were home. Sometimes she would lie down stretching herself out as far as she could soaking up the sun shine, she loved to sun bathe.

Everywhere we traveled with Maddie, we were always asked the same question. Why didn't she have a long tail? On more than one occasion she would get laughed at for not having a long flowing tail. We'd just say she loved to rub against things to itch herself. Her personality more than made up for her lack of a long tail and eventually we did get her to let her tail almost grow down to her knees. But she just never did have much of a tail and you know what? I don't think she really cared!

You often hear the expression of having a "bomb proof" horse. Although I think any well trained horse can have a bad hair day, Maddie was darn close to being just that. Over the years we really didn't notice anything that seemed to bother her. Walking in a wagon train with cars driving by at 50 miles per hour, children crawling and pulling all over her, unusual objects, nothing really bothered her. In her later years we did noticed that she didn't like loud or sharp sounds, but age may have played a part in that and her hearing became more sensitive to sounds. We noticed Woody, Peanut and Brie also were more sensitive to louder sounds as they aged.

Maddie would meet several thousand children as an ambassador for the ranch sharing her gift of unconditional love with them. Whether she was sharing a first ride with a class of special needs children, visiting a child's home for a birthday party or meeting children at a kid's expo, she waited patiently for every child to have an opportunity to sit in her saddle or pet her. Her visits to nursing homes rekindled countless stories of growing up with horses. We would hear so many wonderful stories from individuals remembering using horses on their family farm or how their grandparents rode horses to school.

On a visit to an area nursing home, an individual asked if he could sit on Maddie and he told the story of how horses had played an important part in his life. The gentleman was in his late eighties and with a little assistance he sat in the saddle and asked to have his picture taken. A year later we returned to the nursing home and the gentleman we had met was now unfortunately in a wheel chair. We walked Maddie over to him so he could pet her and feed her an apple and his daughter mentioned he still had that photo by his night stand. If our horses can help create a smile and a memory we can't ask for anything else. We are blessed to share them with others.

Maddie loved to be the center of attention whenever she could and if given the opportunity would gladly show you how to open a door. No matter where she would be around the ranch all we would have to do is call her name and ask if she wanted her grain and she would meander up to the gate softly nickering. If we needed a horse to greet a visitor to the ranch we'd just call her name and she'd walk right up to us.

For all the wonderful memories she gave us, I think we will always cherish her favorite thing she loved to do. Walking up to the old milk house door and opening it with her mouth and then sneaking inside for a little extra senior feed. Seeing a horse half way sticking out the door, we knew it could only be one horse. Good old Maddie.

Good Bye to Maddie

For nearly a year, we had known this day would eventually come and we would have to let a very special horse begin her journey across the Rainbow Bridge. Maddie's arthritis in her right front knee would be too much for her if we had a difficult winter. We had been dealing with her arthritis for the past few years and our vet didn't feel she was in any real pain. For the past two years we had been using a natural holistic product to treat Maddie's arthritis and it was mixed into her daily morning's grain mix. Maddie still loved to walk out to the pastures and spend the day with the other horses and she loved to just lie down soaking up the sun. Maddie was given a special senior grain mix four times a day since her four back molar teeth were gone and her other teeth were very worn.

Whenever she wanted her grain she would walk up to the gate nickering several times as she approached it to let us know she was coming. If we didn't get to the gate soon enough for her, she would just open the gate and let herself in. Maddie was quite the sneak when it came to opening a gate or door. She had developed the knack to use her lips and teeth to turn a door knob or gate latch. For years, if given the opportunity and she didn't think we were anywhere in sight, she would walk over to the milk house we had converted into storage for our feed supplies and casually grasp the door latch and with a few seconds she would be standing half way into the milk house enjoying the nearest bag of grain she could reach.

I remember one day when she had tried to open the door and I thought I'd play a trick on her. The milk house had two entrances, a main door and a side door closer to the barn. As Maddie started walking up to the door, I decided to sneak into the side door so when she opened the door I would be standing there waiting for her. She opened the door and I asked her if I could help her with anything and then I'd close the door. She'd reopen the door and we would repeat this several times. Finally I closed the door and was waiting for Maddie to open it again when I heard a noise behind me. Maddie had decided she would walk around to the side door and just walked right in. She was given some extra treats for that one!

Sue and I had made the decision in early spring that this would be Maddie's last year with us. She also had developed an enlarged thyroid which could keep her from maintaining her weight. So we let her enjoy the next few months hanging out in the pasture with her best friend Brie and opening a few doors whenever she wanted to. As fall approached we were spending more time with Maddie and we knew she could sense something was different, which made the situation all the more difficult to prepare for. I had called the vet several days earlier to schedule the day we had decided to say goodbye.

This would be one of the most difficult days at the ranch that Sue and I would be faced with and it would turn out to be another lesson we learned from the interaction with horses. Sue had always been present to comfort and hold the horses when it was time for them to make their journey across the Rainbow Bridge. But we had decided that it would be better if she would not be here when Dr. Laura arrived. Carissa, one of our volunteers, had asked to come out to the ranch so she could spend some time with Maddie and groom her.

Maddie spent the morning eating her grain and munching on hay with some of the other horses and walked around the pasture with Brie and Penny. Then a really strange thing happened. Maddie lifted her head up from eating and looked off towards the west and then walked into the barn. Within a few minutes Dr. Laura drove around the curve in the road about a quarter of a mile from the ranch, coming from the west. I met her at the gate and we talked about where we would put Maddie to sleep. As we talked, I realized Maddie hadn't come out of the barn and I said I would go get her. Upon entering the barn I found Maddie standing in a corner looking away from the door. When I walked up to her to put her halter on, she slowly turned her head towards me letting me slide her halter over her ears. I rubbed her neck and nose and told her we loved her as I walked her outside. Suddenly Maddie stopped walking with me and didn't want to go any farther. I offered her some of her favorite horse treats and she still didn't want to move. I'm sure she could sense something unusual and she stared over towards the gate where Dr. Laura had been standing.

Some of the horses were still munching on the hay from their morning feeding and as I walked Maddie over to the gate leading to a small grassy area a few of them lifted their heads and softly nickered to Maddie. Maddie didn't want to walk with me and just stopped in her tracks. I tried to coax her forward gently tugging on her lead rope and she would not budge. After rubbing her neck for a few moments, I decided to try and turn her away from the gate and walk away from it. With a little nudge she turned and walked slowly with me and I reached into my pocket and gave her a treat. She pushed on my arm and I gave her a few more treats. Rubbing on her neck I asked her to turn around and we walked slowly towards the gate. As I opened the gate and we walked through it, Maddie turned towards the other horses and nickered several times to them. We walked over to the grassy area and Maddie started to nibble on some grass as Dr. Laura prepared the injections. I lifted Maddie's head up and rubbed her neck and kissed her nose. I told her it was time for her to see Woody again and that she was a very special girl. I could feel the tears starting to run down my face as I asked Dr. Laura to help Maddie on her journey. As I rubbed her mane I told her someday we would see her again. After Dr. Laura had left I noticed Brie had become very upset and nervous and was running from the barn yard area to the pasture franticly nickering in a high pitch voice. She ran back and forth several times running the complete area of the pasture and into the barn. After a few seconds she would run out of the barn with her head raised in the air frantically calling out for an old friend. Brie knew something had happened to Maddie and didn't know where she was or why she hadn't walked back with me through the gate.

I walked over to Brie and told her everything would be alright as I rubbed her neck, but she was still very nervous. I put a halter and lead rope on Brie and walked her over to where Maddie was resting and Brie started to make several soft sounds that I had never heard her make before. She sniffed around Maddie's head and neck and then stood near her for several minutes. Brie started to eat some grass in the small pasture while I buried Maddie and she seemed to be at ease now that she was able to say good bye to an old friend. After I had finished burying Maddie I let Brie sniff the ground and we walked back to the other horses.

You often hear people say that something seemed weird or strange and it was like having a sixth sense. Perhaps in the equine language that horses use to communicate with each other, they may also have a sixth sense.

Dusty Toes

Dusty is small pony about 40" high at the shoulders and he is a bay color with a thick mane and tail. A father called us explaining they had bought a pony for their daughter and that she had now outgrown him. They had tried selling him, but no one had shown any interest in him. If we were interested in him, we could just pick him up. It was about a fifteen minute drive to their dairy farm so I thought I would take the trailer along in case I would be bringing Dusty home with me. Upon pulling into the long driveway leading to the house and barn I could see a little pony tied up near a tree. The parents met me as I was getting out of the truck and we walked over to where Dusty was nibbling on some grass. The first thing I noticed was he hadn't had his feet trimmed in sometime and his hooves looked like he was wearing small clown shoes. He had also floundered at some time and when he walked it was as if you were walking on a carton of eggs trying not to break any of them. Otherwise he had a healthy coat, bright eyes, had been well fed and loved attention. I knew Dusty would fit right in meeting school children. I opened the trailer door and Dusty jumped right in and started eating some of the hay flakes I had put in the trailer.

I called our ferrier as soon as we unloaded Dusty to set up an appointment to get his feet trimmed. We also contacted our veterinarian and asked them to take a look at his hooves. After a lengthy trimming session Dusty could walk on his feet without leaning way back on his heels. Every time Sarah stops by to trim the horses, we also check Dusty toes.

Dusty fit right in with the other horses and he became pals with Peanut and started shadowing him around the pastures and eating next to him. Within a few days they were best friends, grooming on each other and cruising through the open gate to walk along the fence line by the neighbor's driveway to eat grass. When it was time for a drink, Peanut would be walking towards the gate and Dusty would be a few yards behind him. And then it was off through the gate again until we called them to come in for the night.

Dusty enjoys some "Good Eats"

We worked with Dusty for a couple of weeks getting him use to what he might have happen to him when we visited the school classes. Rolling a ball against his feet bothered him at first, but after a few times he actually would bump it back to us. He stood perfectly still when we tugged on his mane and tail and crawled underneath him. Loud sounds or strange objects also didn't upset him, so it was time to visit the schools.

Maddie or Brie we're the two large horses we always brought to the schools so the older kids could ride a horse and then we would bring a pony for the small kids to enjoy. Dusty quickly learned it was fun going to school. Where else would he get all the apples and carrots he could eat for two hours? The kids would brush him and take him for walks around the parking lot helping me hold the lead rope as we gave everyone a ride. Then we would unsaddle Dusty and he would get brushed again and help mow the lawn. Dusty didn't eat grass when he visited schools, the kids would tell us he was helping to mow the lawn. During the next few years that we were involved with an animal assisted therapy program at a local public school system Dusty would become a popular little fellow.

As I mentioned earlier, Dusty and Peanut became the very best of friends. When we would get near the ranch coming back from a visit to a school, Dusty would start calling to Peanut and he would run over to the driveway to greet Dusty as he walked out of the trailer. We'd open the pasture gate and Dusty would roll in the grass and Peanut would wait for him to get up and off they would go side by side. Or they would stand by the gate asking if they could go for a walk along their favorite fence line. Sometimes we'd look to see where they would be eating along the fence line and every now and then we would start to panic because we could not see them right away. They would be laying down sunning themselves and if we would walk out by them you could hear one or both of them snoring.

The day we had to say good bye to Peanut, Dusty could sense something was wrong. He stood near Peanut and he was very nervous and he would not let any of the other horses near the area where Peanut was laying down. After we said good bye to Peanut we let the other horses walk over to him and sniff his body before we buried him. Dusty slowly walked over to him sniffing around his neck and head and then he softly nickered to Peanut. We buried Peanut under a tree not far from the pasture and Dusty could see where he was buried. For the next few days I noticed Dusty would be standing in the corner of the barn yard looking in a certain direction. I'd fill the water tanks and put the hay in the feed bunk without giving it much thought. Everyday I'd rub Dusty on the neck and say I knew how much he missed his best friend. Then it hit me like a brick! Dusty was looking over in the direction of the tree where we had buried Peanut. For the next several weeks we watched Dusty and he would spend hours staring in the direction of that tree. After staring at the tree, he would slowly walk out into the pasture and stand by himself. For several months he wouldn't really interact with any of the other horses. He would walk out with Maddie to eat along the fence line, but he would be the first one to come in and walk up to the gate. Eventually Dusty joined up with our two Belgian draft horses and began interacting with other horses.

Do horses have a sense of emotions? We'll let you decide.

Brie's Bunch

A few years after bringing Maddie home we received a phone call from her previous owner. She explained her parents had sold all their horses but one and were trying to find a good home for her. Since we had purchased Maddie from them they were wondering if we would be interested in another horse with a personality just like Maddie had. Brie was a chocolate colored Grullo Quarter horse and had been in the pasture when we bought Maddie home. We made plans to drive down to their farm and would stop by her father's veterinary clinic to meet him. Upon arriving at the clinic, his wife explained he was still out on a farm call and we should go ahead and look at Brie ourselves. If we decided we wanted her, we could load her up and stop by the clinic on our way back. She also mentioned there were two donkeys that her husband had rescued from an area farm and wondered if we would we be interested in them. I won't repeat what Sue thought about that idea especially with what we were about to go through.

As we pulled into the driveway, we could see Brie and the two donkeys in a small pasture by the barn. The sky was getting darker and it looked like it could start raining at any minute. I remembered it took me nearly a half hour just to chase Maddie from the same pasture into the barn yard. So I hoped this time things would go a little smoother since it had now begun to thunder. We opened the gate and walked towards Brie calling her name and she walked right over to us. She was a very gentle horse and we could tell right away she would be great with our animal assisted therapy activities visiting children with special needs at area elementary schools. We put her halter on and she jumped right into the trailer. Sue and I were relieved things went so well since it now had begun to lightly sprinkle.

The two donkeys, Anna Belle and Jenny had been together for several years before they joined Brie on the farm. They seemed very friendly and in good health, but there was just one problem. You couldn't catch the darn long eared things. And to make matters worse, the light sprinkle had turned into a downpour. Anna Belle and Jenny didn't like the rain, so we able to get them inside an open area of the barn after they ran circles around the truck and trailer deciding they weren't going to jump in by Brie. After an hour of trying everything we could think of to get halters on them, including apple slices, sweet feed and horse treats we tried to use Brie as bait. The trailer door had been open during this circus and Brie would whinny to the donkeys but they had no interest in getting into the trailer. We untied Brie and tried walking her around and leading the donkeys into the trailer and that didn't work. We let Brie walk into the trailer by herself and that didn't work. We put sweet feed on the trailer floor hoping they would jump in and that didn't work, but Brie sure enjoyed that idea. Finally, as Sue was just about to shoot me, I said the heck with it we are just taking Brie and we'll leave the donkeys here. Ten seconds after putting Brie in the trailer Anna Belle and Jenny jumped in the trailer like they were shot out of a cannon. Sue got into the truck and once again I can not repeat what she said to me. Being soaking wet probably didn't help the cause. We stopped by the clinic to let them know we had all three loaded and we picked up their vaccination records.

It was a little more than an hour drive back to the ranch and we stopped about half way home to get some gas and check on the troops to see how they were riding. I think anyone that was at that gas station on that day could still tell you a good story. As I was filling the gas tank I started to talk to Anna Belle and Jenny and that's all it took. They started to bray together and I swear five minutes later they hadn't come up for air yet. From inside the stock trailer they decided to have a braying contest that lasted the entire time we were there. Everyone was laughing and pointing towards the trailer. As Sue sunk down in her seat, I paid for the gas and we headed for home and I believe Sue said they most likely would never let us back at that gas station again.

As we pulled into the driveway Brie started whinnying in a high pitch and we noticed Maddie had run over to the gate and was also whinnying and pacing up and down the fence. Brie was anxious in the trailer and was moving back and forth and of course Anna Belle and Jenny had to get their two cents in and started braying. We unloaded the donkeys into a round pen to let them get familiar with everything. We untied Brie and she jumped out of the trailer and pulled us towards the fence where Maddie was waiting. They quickly smelled each other's nose and almost immediately started grooming on each other's necks over the fence. Sue and I had wondered if Brie and Maddie would remember each other and as we found out later, they had been pasture buddies for a few years before we purchased Maddie. We took the halter off of Brie and let her and Maddie run off into the pasture with Peanut and Rusty close behind.

Brie settled right in, with Maddie close by her side and Woody right next to her. Anna Belle and Jenny weren't bothered by anything and would become the ranch clowns entertaining everyone that visited the ranch. So despite getting soaked and getting some strange looks at the gas station we knew we made the right decision bringing Brie's bunch home.

Brie enjoys the holidays with a volunteer

Brie was a very quiet horse. Her personality was easy going and she wasn't bothered by anything. She would trail ride anywhere and wasn't afraid of traffic or unusual sounds.

We worked with her for a couple of weeks getting her used to what she would have to deal with when she visited the schools. We pushed on her all over her body, grabbed her mane and tail, and bounced a rubber ball near her and on her back and rump. We bumped her legs with our feet and pushed a lawn chair and cart by her legs and bumped into them as we walked her around them. I also got on my hands and knees and crawled under her from one side to another and between her front legs. Brie just stood there wondering what the heck I was doing to her. Brie was ready to go for a ride to visit our special friends at school.

I unloaded Brie in the parking lot of the elementary school we visited every week and put her saddle on while the children were coming out of the door. As the children yelled out in excitement "it's a horse", they walked (or should I say ran) over to meet Brie. Brie was a real trooper letting the kids mug her. She was getting her tail pulled, getting brushed from three different directions, had someone sitting in the saddle and trying to eat an apple treat all at once and she just absolutely loved it. Each child was given the opportunity to go for a ride on Brie as I led her with a lead rope, and a couple of children would walk along with me helping to hold onto the lead rope.

Over the next few years, Brie would bring some pretty big smiles to over one hundred children a week visiting our special need friends. She really enjoyed going to schools, you could see the glow in her eyes when the children were around her.

Like Maddie, Brie had also learned to open doors and gates unknown to us. We wondered if Brie would take the place of Maddie opening doors and it wouldn't take long to find out. If a gate was left unlocked for a few seconds and Brie was around, she would nudge it open with her nose to follow you. One particular gate had a latch hook on it and Brie had figured out that if she nudged the gate back and forth with her nose several times, she could get the latch to pop open. Then she would push the gate open and walk right in. She also learned to walk over to where we kept the grain for the horses and she would take tap the door with one of her front legs trying to get attention. But Brie will always be remembered for just walking over to that gate that we used to let everyone in for their special treats and just stand there and nicker in a soft voice waiting for us to let her in. If we didn't let her in right away, she would begin to nicker a little louder. And if that didn't work she would walk around you in circles trying to head you towards the gate if you were trying to ignore her. That was always a fun game to play with her; she would take her head and neck and try to nudge you in the direction of the gate. If Brie was out in the pasture or just meandering around somewhere all you had to do was ask her if she wanted her grain and she would walk up to get her grain.

Brie was given a senior grain mix several times a day because her teeth were so worn down. Her back molar teeth were so worn down they were nearly non-existent. The last few years when Brie munched on grass, she would chew it and then drop it out of her mouth looking like a tobacco plug. So we supplemented her diet with natural supplements mixed into a senior feed mix for the last few years of her life and she loved to let us know when she wanted her grain.

Brie was a great ambassador for the ranch; greeting groups when they visited. She would just walk right up to me when I would be talking to groups about the ranch as if she was waiting to be introduced. And she loved to play the loose tooth game with children. We would talk to groups about caring for horses and Brie loved the attention as we demonstrated what we could do with her. I'd crawl underneath her as I was talking or would walk behind her leaning on her rump and then would lean backwards holding onto her tail illustrating how calm and gentle Brie was. Then I would show them her teeth and mention I noticed she had a loose tooth. I'd ask everyone if they wanted me to pull it out so they could see what a horse tooth looked like. As everyone yelled yes, I gave Brie an apple to eat and then slide my fingers inside her lips and pretended to pull at a tooth. Slowly I opened my hand and there was a big molar tooth from a horse fresh with apple juice on it. The children and some adults couldn't believe that Brie just lost a tooth. Then I would explain that the molar tooth was from Maddie when she had dental surgery. I can recall several times that when we'd all count "one-two-three" and I would pull my hand from Brie's mouth and a couple of adults were turning a little white. One year a first grade teacher started to feel a little faint and had to sit down for a few minutes. Brie just took everything in stride when school groups visited the ranch or we visited the schools. She would just stand quietly until the last child had a chance to brush her. She always was given a couple of apples when we were done and a big bowl of grain when we returned to the ranch.

Brie loved to go for rides and given the opportunity she would break into a gallop. Just about the time you thought she was going as fast as she could, you could feel her body kick it up one more notch and she would fly across an open field. Her previous owner had mentioned that she loved to run and Brie truly did. Even into her early thirties, Brie would still want to go for a gallop if given the opportunity. And like Maddie, Brie had learned to respond to voice and hand signals. When we would visit senior citizen centers or nursing homes we would ask Brie to stand and then give her a hand signal as we told her to stay. Then we would walk a several yards away from her and ask her to come to us and she would walk right over to us. She would be so gentle walking around an individual in a wheel chair and letting them rub her neck, that no one would believe me when telling the story of how Brie could run like the wind.

During the later years of Brie's life, she started to develop an enlarged thyroid problem. When we first noticed Brie's thyroid might be getting larger, it felt about the size of a large marble and we'd check it every month and we'd have Dr. Laura check it whenever she was at the ranch. Slowly her thyroid continued to grow and we knew it could eventually affect her ability to maintain her weight. We made the decision to let Brie enjoy one more summer and fall at the ranch and then it would be time for her to be reunited with Maddie. Carissa, one of our teenage volunteers, had spent the past four years with Brie and she understood the decision that we had to make. She had grown very attached to Brie over the years and whenever we visited a nursing home, senior citizen center or had a group visiting the ranch she would be there whenever possible to introduce everyone to Brie. Carissa could spend hours just lying on Brie bareback as she meandered around the pasture or grooming and braiding her mane and tail. Sometimes when we didn't know where she had gone, all we had to do was look for Brie and she would be lying on Brie with her arms hugging Brie's neck.

Carissa had asked Sue and me if she could come out to the ranch the day we would decide to say goodbye to Brie. We talked about what we would do with Dr. Laura on that day and it would be her decision. Carissa wanted to spend a few hours with Brie grooming her mane and tail before Dr. Laura arrived. A few tears were shed by all of us as we spent time brushing her. Carissa hugged Brie and gave her a kiss on her nose. I patted her neck and hugged her while thanking her for being such a good horse. We removed Brie's halter and kissed her on her nose one last time and she was buried next to her pasture mate of so many years so she could be reunited with Maddie.

Memories of Brie will bring smiles as we remember her racing across an open field and her visits to schools and nursing homes. Brie was thirty six years old when she started her journey across the Rainbow Bridge.

Slice

For several years we had a small petting zoo for making appearances for commercial businesses, corporate picnics or church picnics. We usually had a couple of goats, a llama, rabbits, a couple of horses and a calf as part of the exhibit. Everyone loved to help bottle feed a calf, so we usually purchased a young calf just learning to drink from a bottle from an area dairy farmer. For years we always had boy cows, since most dairy farmers would ship them shortly after being born.

A couple of years after we stopped traveling with our petting zoo, we had a call from a local restaurant asking if we could do a small petting zoo for a Father's Day promotion. Because they used a cow theme throughout the restaurant, they asked if we could bring a calf. I stopped by an area farmer that we knew to see if they had any calves they were getting ready to ship that we could buy for this event. It just so happened that they just had a set of twins born a couple of weeks earlier and were getting ready to have them picked up by a local livestock dealer. The twins were a boy and girl, so there would be a high probability that neither one would mature as an adult. Opposite twins are usually sterile so they had also planned on shipping the female. Since we had never had a girl calf, we decided to take the little girl. Since all the calves had been given names after my golf game, we needed to decide on a name. Previous names used were Bogey, Divot, Mulligan and Fore. After giving careful thought to my golfing skills, we decided to name our new calf Slice. And as they say, the rest would be history and our lives would be changed forever.

We quickly came to learn that Slice would love getting her "ba-ba". Sue would always ask Slice if she wanted her "ba-ba" of milk instead of her bottle of milk. As a calf, Slice had the head and neck shape of a bull calf. She had a thick neck and brisket and whenever someone saw her for the first time, they'd always ask how old the bull calf was. Slice would soon become the hit of the petting zoo. She would lie down on a pile of hay and fall asleep with her head tucked into her side, then she would wake up after taking a short nap and Sue would ask if she wanted her favorite thing. Sue would mix the milk replacement with some warm water and the show would start. Slice would walk over to Sue and with a couple of nudges on the bottle with her nose the feeding frenzy was on.

Slice

We always had two bottles for Slice to drink and if you didn't hold her bottle just right, she'd give the bottle a head butt. Everyone would laugh when Slice would send the bottle flying out of our hands and then started dancing with her front feet until we retrieved the bottle from the ground. We'd help children hold the bottle for

Slice so they could help feed her and we could feel when it was just the right time to have them take a step to the side as Slice neared the end of the bottle and would push up against the rubber nipple for the last few drops of milk.

For some reason, we never trained Slice to walk with a calf halter. We tried putting one on her a couple of times and she would pull back and twist her head from side to side trying to get it off. Instead we put a large dog collar around her neck attached to a lead rope and for whatever the reason, she loved to walk along when we put the collar on her.

It would only be a few short months before she outgrew the dog collars and we had to get her a regular cow collar from the local farm suppler. Slice quickly became the pet around the ranch and she was allowed to meander where ever she wanted to go. Some days, she would walk out to the pasture with the horses and other days she would just lie near the barn in the sun catching a few rays.

Slice quickly learned her name and wherever she would be around the ranch, we'd just have to call her name and she would come slowly strolling up to us. This would prove to save her life a few years later. She also learned to recognize the sound of Sue's car and when Sue would be getting close to the ranch from working, Slice would walk over to our gate to greet her.

When we offered field trips for schools and other organizations, we'd have some of the animals in pens for everyone to look at and we'd give Slice her ba-ba to show the children how a calf drank her bottle of milk everyday. Then one day the funniest thing happened after we gave Slice her two bottles of milk. We had finished talking about Slice and were walking over to look at some of the other animals, when we heard a loud noise behind us. Slice decided we weren't finished with her and started pushing the four sided twelve foot long panels she was in towards us. She was about nine months old by this time and after realizing she could move the panels around by pushing them with her head, there was only one thing we could do. Release the Beast! From that day forward, Slice became an ambassador to the ranch and when groups arrived for their visit, she would greet them at the gate. Slice would just stand next to me and as the children would walk by, they would pet her and she would just stand there enjoying the attention. On a warm sunny day, Slice would plop down to work on her tan and the children would walk up to her and she would just get mugged. Kids would be petting her head, rubbing her ears and trying to sit on her. We soon realized that we could have several children sit on Slice for a photo opportunity and she would just sit there. Of course it helped to give her a hamburger bun or cookie for a reward treat.

Sue always kept Slice's bottle in one of our storage areas so it was easy to get to when we needed it. Sue's mother would often come out to the ranch to help get things ready for an upcoming group visit and sometimes stay to help with the tour. Then one day another funny thing happened; I guess this would depend on what side of the door you were on. We were cleaning up after a school group had visited us and suddenly Sue's mother disappeared. I was filling water tanks and starting to grain some of the horses when I realized I hadn't seen Lois in awhile. I didn't think anything of it, she could be inside our pole shed or sometimes she liked to walk over to the fence and feed the horses apples or bread slices. After about half an hour I thought I heard a faint voice calling out, but I never really gave it a second thought. Then as I was walking through the pole shed, I heard this voice calling out, "Help, get me out of here. Wes, get me out of here. Get this *#@# cow out of here." As I walked around our pole shed, Slice was leaning against the storage room door with her front legs locked forward and her head against the door. I asked Slice what she was doing and suddenly I heard Lois from the other side of the storage door repeat those famous words, "Get that #*@# cow out of here." Slice thought she was going to get her ba-ba and was so excited she leaned against the door pinning Lois inside. It could have been worse; Slice only had Lois pinned inside the room for 30 minutes. From that day on, Lois never went in the storage room again.

One day I received a phone call from the county sheriff's office asking me if I could leave work and get out to the ranch as soon as possible. One of the county sheriff officers was a member of the same church we were and he was driving by the ranch when he noticed something. Slice was fairly athletic in her younger days and she had jumped over our 42" high picket fence that we had around the ranch and she was lying in the grass by the driveway. When I pulled into the driveway Slice was lying down busy chewing her cud and the sheriff officer was leaning against his squad car a few feet away. They say a picture is worth a thousand words and I think this one would have been worth a little more than that. I opened the gate not far from Slice and called her name asking her to get up. Slice slowly got up grabbed another mouth full of grass and walked through the gate heading for the water tank.

We had the vet stop by the ranch one day to give our sheep and goats their yearly de-worming medication when Slice happened to wander by. Just for a fluke idea I asked if we could check Slice to see of she had developed into a mature cow. After examining her for a few minutes, he smiled and said she had all her parts. A few days later I ran into a friend who I helped milk cows for on their farm whenever they needed an extra hand and he mentioned they had the artificial inseminator coming to their farm to breed some heifers for them. So I stopped by and asked him what he had that would we could use to breed Slice with and he suggested using some generic semen that he used to bred young heifers with. After he had finished at our neighbor's farm, he stopped by and we had Slice bred. If the cow accepts the breeding, around the fortieth day you can do a pregnancy check to see if the cow had been bred. So we patiently counted down the days when our vet would stop by to see if Slice would become a mother. The day finally arrived and our vet stopped by to see if Slice was pregnant and within a few minutes he jokingly announced we were going to be grandparents. Slice had grown up to be a big girl, meaning she didn't miss any meals and we could only wonder how big she would get carrying a calf for 9 months and 9 days. The days and weeks flew by and suddenly it was getting close to Slice's delivery date so we started to check her udders for signs of discharging milk when we squeezed them. On the morning of the 9th month and 9th day as if by clockwork, it was time for Slice to give birth. Around 6 a.m., Sue had noticed Slice walking around licking at her stomach and getting a little irritated. She was walking around in a circle arching her back and continued to lick her stomach. About an hour later, Slice broke her water bag and laid down. Sue quickly called me at work and it would take me about 20 minutes to get home, so I hoped everything would go according to plan until I got home. When I arrived home, Sue was sitting on the ground next to Slice rubbing her stomach trying to keep her calm and we decided to call the vet right away explaining we had an emergency. The clinic opened at 7 a.m., so when I called we didn't have to go through the answering service and we were able to get one of the vets to come right out. We knew they should arrive within 30 minutes, about the same time we had a group of volunteers from an area correctional institute arriving for a day of community service. As the vet pulled into our driveway, the van carrying the group of Drug Abuse Correctional Center (D.A.C.C.) volunteers, helping with projects on the ranch, was right behind him. The individuals enrolled in this program and if they successfully completed it they were given an earlier release date of whatever sentencing they were given. It was a good group of individuals, but a couple of the guys didn't like to be near each other because they were from the same large city and were members of intercity opposing gangs. If fact, if they would see each other on the streets a fight or something worse could result in their meeting on the streets. I told them they might be helping deliver the birth of a calf this morning. The vet quickly determined the calf was backwards and had become stuck in the delivery process and he could barely reach it, so there was no chance of trying to help deliver the calf without performing an emergency C section.

A C-section is usually preformed with the cow standing and today we would need the assistance of everyone to help keep Slice from wanting to lie down. As the vet prepared Slice for the C-section, he asked if everyone could stand on the opposite side of Slice from her head to tail to help hold her up. After the area was clipped and blocked to help freeze the area the incision would be made everyone gathered around Slice to help keep her standing up. Some of the guys had only seen a horse or cow on T.V. until they visited the ranch, so this was about to become a real learning experience for several of them. The vet made an incision about 18" long just passed Slice's rib cage on her right side cutting through the hide and inner muscle and fat areas. He then reached inside Slice's side to make the final incision to where he could try and reach the calf. While this was happening a couple of the guys were looking a little on the faint side and the two individuals that had no contact with each other when in their unit at D.A.C.C., were standing next to each other with their arms locked with each and leaning against Slice shoulder to shoulder talking to each other about what they should do next and what was happening.

The vet could barely reach the calf and he had to strain to feel how the legs were positioned. The calf was backwards and the only way it could be delivered was by pulling it out hind feet first. Once the vet was able to get the hind feet through the incision, we helped hold the calf as he continued to pull the calf out. This sure seemed to be one long calf as we waited for the head and front feet to emerge. Slowly the hind legs and body appeared and with one final pull, the front shoulder appeared and then the head and front legs slide through the incision. All stretched out from his hind feet to the front feet the calf was taller than me and I'm over 6 feet tall. Sue and a couple of friends that came out to watch the birth quickly grabbed several towels and started drying the calf off as three of the guys helped hold him as he laid on the ground. The rest of the group continued to hold Slice while the vet returned everything to where it belonged inside Slice and sewed the incision closed. The vet thought it would be about an hour before the calf would be up and around after everything it had had been through. To the surprise of everyone, the vet hadn't finished with the last stitch on Slice's incision and the calf was trying to get up. After three or four unsuccessful attempts and falling in the straw, the little guy not only got up, but started to bounce around hopping and running in all directions. He suddenly came to a stop wondering where the heck he was and then made a direct bee line to Slice as she gave out a soft mooing sound. In a matter of seconds the calf was trying to find the milk faucets. Unfortunately they weren't located between Slice's front legs. With a little assistance the calf soon figured things out and barely came up for air. Slice would become a great mother and never let her calf wander off to far without calling him back. After a few weeks we let Slice and her calf out of the box stall we had built for her to venture out into the pastures as we walked along with them. The calf would run around Slice without a care in the world and suddenly find himself running into the side of a horse. The horses really didn't pay much attention to their new friend, in fact a couple of the Shetland ponies would run around with the calf as if to be playing tag. Sometimes the calf would chase the horses and then the horses would chase the calf under the watchful eye of Slice.

While Slice was giving birth, the social worker that brought the group to the ranch was taking photos of the entire event. Several of the guys asked if they could have copies of the photos to send to their family members, many who also had never seen a cow up close and personal. For several years, photos of the D.A.C.C. guys helping with Slice's delivery were on the bulletin board in the lobby of their unit. Slice and her calf had helped individuals build their self esteem and communication skills through their interactions with an animal and I think on that day, everyone learned what the gift of unconditional love truly was. The two individuals from rival street gangs stood next to each other exchanging high-fives. During the remainder of the summer, the group came out to the ranch every couple of weeks and the first thing they wanted to see or ask about was Slice and her calf.

One day we had one of our youth volunteers at the ranch. I had just returned from riding and, for whatever reason, said sometime we should put a saddle on Slice. Without any further thought, we unsaddled the horses and before Slice knew what was happening, we had a saddle pad and saddle on her. I held Slice with a rope halter and Cait jumped up in the saddle and from that day forward whenever we asked if anyone wanted to be a cowgirl or cowboy they had the chance to sit on Slice.

Now nearly 10 years old, Slice continues to think she is just an oversized dog. She still greets us at the gate and if offered her "ba-ba" after all these years, she still knows what it is. Slice has acquired a taste for several things over the years including bread, cookies, carrots and fresh beets right out of the garden. She has stopped jumping over fences, weighing close to 2,000 pounds she realizes it's easier to just walk through it. On sunny days she loves to lay in the pasture sunning herself and when it's feeding time, we just have to call her name and slowly but surely she comes meandering up to get a bite of hay. When Sue and I drive around the curve to the ranch, we often see Slice just lying in the pasture chewing her cud as she looks around without a care in the world. She's one happy cow.

Trigger

Trigger arrived at the ranch on a cold day in January several years ago. An individual moved out of state and basically left the horse in the care of a friend. We were asked if we could help out and provide a home for him.

One day while our ferrier was trimming some of the horses, she told us about this crazy horse she was trimming who nearly jumped over her back. She said the horse was just nuts and was thinking about dropping the client because the horse was so unruly and dangerous. This horse was Trigger.

Dr. Laura arrived the day after we had brought Trigger to the ranch to give him a health check for us. We knew he was updated on his vaccinations since the individual had used the same vet clinic that we did. Trigger was in fairly good health and we found out he was a cryptorchid or, in other words, he only had one developed testicle. There was a very good chance that the other testicle was still trapped near his kidney and stomach area. The clinic didn't perform the special surgery that Trigger would need, so Dr .Laura suggested calling a clinic near Green Bay, Wisconsin. We called the clinic and explained the situation with Trigger and asked if they could help us. We spoke with someone in the equine clinic and they explained how the surgery would be preformed and they would keep Trigger a couple of days after the surgery to make sure his recovery was off to good start. I opened the trailer door and Trigger walked right in with me, although I'm sure that if he knew where we were headed he would not have been so anxious to jump in the trailer.

It was about an hour and a half drive to the clinic and they wanted Trigger to be there the day before surgery so he would be rested from the drive. I arrived at the clinic around 3:30 in the afternoon and we put Trigger in a box stall for the night. He would be operated on around 9:00 the following morning. I gave him a couple of carrots and rubbed his nose. I told him I'd see him in a couple of days. I called the clinic around noon the following day to see how everything went and they said they found the testicle pinned between the kidney and the stomach area and he was doing fine. We were relieved that everything went well and now as a gelding, perhaps Trigger's personality would take a turn for the better.

If given the opportunity he would try to spin around in his box stall and think about kicking you. When on a lead rope, it wasn't uncommon for Trigger to stop and rear up kick at the lead rope. Then just for good measure he would throw in a couple of bunny hops. Walking next to you on a lead rope wasn't one of his favorite things to do either, but I don't think he was ever shown what was expected of him or taught any manners. He thought he could walk all over you and was just a pushy horse to say the least. So we were hoping I would be bringing home a changed horse personality wise.

Trigger spending time in the Garden

I called the clinic and the receptionist said they wanted to keep Trigger one more day; they wanted the swelling to go down a little more, but I could plan on picking him up the next day. When we walked over to his stall, Trigger eagerly ate the carrots I had brought along and he was more then ready to get out of Dodge. The doctor who performed the surgery said he was a good patient and everything went as they had hoped it would. He suggested that we keep him in a box stall for a couple of weeks, keep an eye on the swelling and watch for any additional drainage from his stitches. We had already called Dr. Laura to set up an appointment to check Trigger in a few days. Once we arrived back home I think he was glad to spend the next few days in his stall. We would get him out for a little exercise twice a day and then it was back into his stall. After two weeks, we let Trigger out with the other horses for a few hours to get some exercise during the day and then kept him in the box stall for another week. By the end of the third week, Trigger seemed well on his way to recovery and he would occasionally run with the other horses.

What a difference the surgery had on changing the personality of this once crazy horse! He was now a much calmer horse and was eager to be with you, but he was still on the pushy side with his head and body so we needed to work on that issue. Now when we would enter his box stall, he quickly faced us to see if we had any treats for him. He was learning to walk next to us when using a lead rope and we had begun the basic lessons to help him become a better horse. We quickly saw that he was eager to please us. Once Trigger had learned the basics of stopping when we asked him to, stood still for a few minutes while we rubbed his shoulders and legs and walked next to us like a gentleman should I thought I'd try something else with him.

I had met an international equine clinician who trained horses using food as a reward while teaching the horse to respond to hand and voice commands. So I thought I'd try to teach Trigger to walk next to me using hand and voice signals. I also wanted to see if I could get him to go away from me and then ask him to return to me when asked. Little did I realize this would help us avoid something that could have been a disaster. After several weeks of working with Trigger, he had progressed enough to the point that I would walk him along the shoulder of the road with the lead rope loosely laying across his neck as I lightly held on to it. Then a few months later I think we were both surprised by what happened next. It was December and I had just finished snow blowing a path up to the barn doors when I noticed Trigger was walking along the shoulder of the road towards me. I had forgotten to latch the gate and he pushed it open with his head and decided to go for a walk. Unfortunately there was a car approaching and let's just say the driver was moving right along, showing no signs of slowing down even with a horse on the side of the road. So I ran towards Trigger raising my arms trying to get him to go away from me. To my surprise he came to a stop, looked at me and then suddenly turned and ran about thirty yards into a field next to the road. The car never slowed down and I may have said a few words as they sped by. Now I had to figure out how to get a horse out of a field with about two feet of snow in it when he was having a blast running in it. I walked about ten yards into the field and thought what the heck have I got to lose. I raised my arms and calling Trigger's name I started to take a few steps backwards. He slowly came to a stop and once again looked at me with both eyes, so I knew I had gotten his attention. Now the rest was up to him. As I slowly walked backwards, Trigger started to trot towards me and came to a halt a few yards from me. I turned away from him asking him to walk with me as I motioned with my arm and hand. He walked up to me and stood at my side while we walked down the road and through the gate. Needless to say, someone was given a bowl of grain when we returned to the round pen.

Trigger continues to learn how to respond to hand and voice signals in preparing him for bridleless riding. The high school volunteers continue to try and jump on his back while he eats his grain; sometimes they succeed, sometimes they don't.

When Sarah arrived to trim some of the horses, I mentioned I had an old friend waiting for her. When she saw who was waiting for her, I really can't repeat what she said. I think she said I was nuts. After Trigger stood almost perfectly still for his trimming, she was shocked and I must admit so was I. His once crooked front legs have straightened out and he has really matured into a very handsome guy. In fact, that is the nickname Sue has given him - handsome.

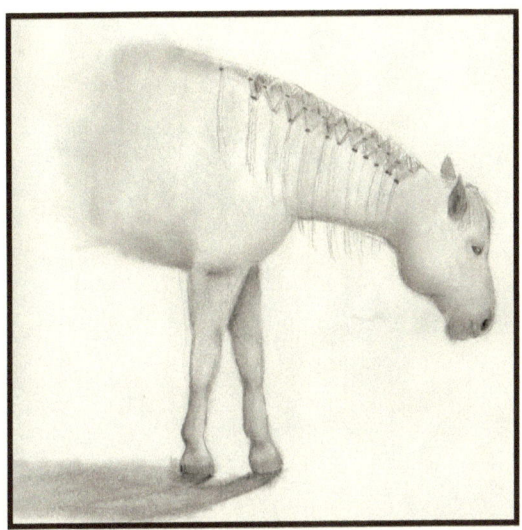

Trigger

As Charles Wilhelm, an equine clinician, states, "It's never ever the horses fault." Trigger is a living example. Trigger has overcome his pushing issues and has learned to respect our space when we interact with him. He has transformed from a horse that once was more than happy to kick you if given the chance, to one of the most loving horses we have today. It was possible all through sharing the gift of unconditional love between two individuals - a human and a horse.

Peter and His Best Pal Patches

Peter is a thoroughbred that arrived at the ranch in May of 2000. He had been abused in Minnesota and was now living in Northwestern Wisconsin. He was in need of a new home and, to make a long story short, he arrived on Memorial Day. Somewhere in his life, Pete was mistreated by being tied to a solid object such as a hitching post and when it came time to loading into a trailer. Over the years he has learned to overcome his two worst fears to some degree. When Peter arrived at the ranch we introduced him to a few of the horses and then let him interact with the entire group of horses. It was clear right away that Peter had "the perfect gentleman syndrome". At feeding time, he would walk around the feed bunk until everyone else had found a spot to eat. If the horse next to him would raise his head, Peter would walk away and find another spot to eat. Walking up to the water tanks, he would do the same thing and wait until everyone had a chance to drink before he would walk up to the tank. Although he is one of the taller horses and could make his presence known if he wanted to cause a fuss, he is right near the bottom of the herd pecking order and seems to be perfectly content.

We often practice loading and unloading some of the horses we use in our animal assisted therapy activities so they are used to jumping in the trailer when we need them to. We thought we'd try loading Peter to see how he would do and it didn't take long to find out. Fifty feet away from the trailer Peter slammed on the brakes and came to a dead stop and then tried to turn away from the trailer. He was deathly afraid of that big dark cave and wanted no part of getting near it. We walked around the trailer and he would be ok with that, but he would snort at the trailer as he walked around it. After several attempts of walking towards the trailer door, Peter would get within thirty feet of the door before he would come to a stop. So off we'd go, walking around the trailer and seeing if we could get him to accidentally walk closer to it. Peter would walk right next to the side of the trailer without any problem, but as soon as we approached the door he was off and pulling you right with him. Eventually, after taking many more steps backwards then forward, Peter walked into the trailer but with great anxiety. To make walking into the trailer a better experience for Peter, we placed three of our horse panels around the back of the trailer door making a small pen area. We put a couple of flakes of hay in the front on the trailer and walked Peter inside the horse panels while we removed his halter. After a few snorts and sticking his head into the trailer a couple of times, Peter slowly put one foot into the trailer and then walked into the trailer to eat the hay. Over the course of an hour or so without even thinking about it, he had walked in and out of the goofy trailer a dozen times. There was enough room in the trailer for Peter to turn around and walk out head first. So whenever we need to take Peter on a road trip, we just take three horse panels along for the ride. And over the years, Peter has also learned that when he walks into the trailer there is a bowl of treats waiting for him.

The other problem that Peter had was that you could not tie him to anything unless you wanted to have a major disaster on your hands. If Peter felt any type of constant pressure against his halter, he would continue to back up until the pressure was released. Someone once tried to saddle Peter while holding the lead rope tightly in their hand and Peter just kept walking in circles backwards. The more they held the rope tightly in their hand, the more Peter would back up. If you just let Peter stand without holding onto the lead rope, you could usually saddle him without any problem. It is always funny to watch individuals try and saddle Peter after you mention the less pressure you use the easier it is to work with Peter. Everyone thinks you have to keep applying pressure to get any type of results. To some extent that might be true, but the important thing is to know when to release the pressure.

When we would use Peter to visit individuals with special needs, you would never know he had a problem with someone pulling on his lead rope. He would let children crawl underneath him and stand like a statue while we helped individuals up into the saddle to go for a ride. We would walk Peter right up to an individual with a wheelchair so they could stand up and get on him to go for a ride and he would never move. When we asked him to be a good boy, he was a very good boy.

At the ranch, Peter met a little guy named Patches and for some reason they have developed a close friendship. Patches is a miniature horse about thirty four inches high at the shoulders. He would interact with the other horses, but didn't really have anyone that he really liked to be with. One day we saw Peter and Patches grooming each other on their neck and they have been best friends ever since. They walk around the pasture together and when we bring Peter in for his special grain mix, someone is walking a few yards behind him. So the little guy gets a little treat also. When we feed in the morning and at night, Peter will walk around looking to see if Patches has found a place to eat. If he hasn't, he will walk next to Patches and together they will find a place to eat next to each other. If their eating spot is disrupted, they will walk off together until they can eat next to each other again. During the night we often walk out into the barn and pasture to see what the horses are doing and Peter and Patches are always next to each other. Patches may be lying down and Peter will be standing over him or they will be laying down right next to each other.

We needed a little guy for our animal assisted therapy activities with the school system we were visiting since the majority of children were between the ages of four and seven years old. Patches would be the perfect fit. Sometimes we would surprise the class we were going to visit and just stroll down the hallway and into the classroom with a horse in tow. Patches was quiet on his feet and you could hardly hear him walking down the hallway on his little hooves. Once inside the classroom we would play "Follow the Leader" and Patches would lead everyone outside. Over the years Patches had his mane and tail pulled, his legs bumped by a wheelchair and a few wet diapers on his back, but through it all Patches was a great horse around the children. Sometimes when we would give him a firm apple to eat, his first bite into the apple would send a spray of apple juice into the air and the children would just laugh. One time when we were taking the elevator up to the second floor of a school as the door opened a waiting teacher was somewhat surprised to see a horse in it and she said a naughty word.

Peter is thirty years old and his best friend Patches is seventeen years old.

Reagan

A year before Reagan arrived at the ranch, we had a phone call from his owner who had found our website while searching for a home for him. I explained to her that we were not taking any additional horses at the time but would try any help her find a home for him and we also gave her the names of some other organizations that might be able to assist her. She was calling from another state and said she was unable to place Reagan with any of the organizations there. Nearly a year later we received an email from her again seeking assistance in finding him a home. She offered to pay for the hay Reagan would eat each month if we could help her.

Reagan

Reagan was being boarded in Wisconsin about an hour drive south of where we were located. I called the number she gave me for the stable where Reagan was being kept and after playing phone tag for several days I spoke with the woman who owned the boarding and training stable. Reagan had been at her facility for the past five years and basically was turned out into a pasture during the day and brought into a box stall for the night. More recently he had been outside 24/7, unless it was going to rain, during the summer months. During the winter he was in a box stall and occasionally turned out for a few hours. The woman explained that for the past few months it was getting increasingly difficult to collect the monthly boarding fees. The first few years a check arrived every month for his care, but she needed to continually call to get her payment and the woman had been a few months behind with her payments. In fact she was two months behind in her payments when we talked on the phone.

We made arrangements for driving down to see Reagan in a couple of weeks. As I pulled into the driveway a women was walking out of the barn with a couple of hay bales on a cart. She was heading up to the pasture where Reagan was to finish his morning feeding. She called out his name and he walked over to the gate and she grabbed a lead rope and clipped it to his halter. We walked him through the gate and over to an area where he could eat some grass. Reagan was an American Warm Blood standing around 16 hands high and he was a bay. He stood quietly as I rubbed his neck and hind quarters and picked up each of his feet. The woman explained he had a navicular injury in one of his front feet, but it only bothered him if he was ridden on a hard surface or for a long period of time. It may cause a slight limp for a couple of days until the tenderness went away. She had him for about five years and some of her students had occasionally ridden him and he didn't show any signs of lameness after they had finished riding him.

The owner of the boarding stable had basically grown tired of dealing with Reagan's owner and had tried to find him a good home. But no one was interested in a horse with a navicular issue. Her husband didn't want her to keep another pasture buddy and wanted the horse gone. I knew we could use Reagan to do some of the things we had done with Maddie, so I opened the trailer door and in he went. Reagan barely fit into the trailer being so tall and I hoped he would be a quiet rider for the trip home. I stopped about half way back to the ranch to see how he was riding and Reagan had turned himself sideways and settled right down.

Upon arriving back at the ranch I opened the trailer door and Reagan wasn't in a rush to leap out of the trailer. He slowly walked to the end of the trailer and stepped right out taking in his new surroundings. Maddie and Brie walked over to the gate to greet the new arrival and they sniffed each others' noses and exchanged a few nickers. I kept Reagan on a lead rope as we walked amongst the other horses giving everyone a chance to walk over and greet the new arrival. This was pretty uneventful so I removed the lead rope from his halter and let him explore the pasture and barn by himself. I walked along several yards behind him just in case things got a little too frisky with the other horses, but no one seemed to care that he had joined the herd. Within a few days, Reagan was meandering around the ranch and interacting with the other horses as if he had been here for years.

One of the surprising things we discovered about Reagan is that he did not like objects raised over the front or top of his head. He had been a successful equestrian jumper before his injury and we just found it odd that he didn't like anything above his head. We used a variety of things to help desensitize Reagan to numerous situations. We used a 36" inflatable ball to roll against his legs and under his stomach. A large plastic tarp was spread out on the ground so he could get use to walking a different surface and the sound he would hear from walking on it. Using a horseman's cane we rubbed his entire body. Touching his ears, back, thigh, legs and hooves with the cane to see how he would react and that is how we discovered his shyness around his head. Using the horseman cane I waved my arm back and forth in the air several feet away from Reagan. If he backed away I'd continue waving until he stopped and then release the pressure of waving the cane and reward him. We repeated this several times until Reagan realized the cane wasn't anything that was going to harm him. Then we bounced the large ball in front of him and rolled it against his front legs. After he was comfortable with this we placed the ball on his back and rolled it back and forth several times without any problem. Letting him smell the ball, we then placed it against both sides of his neck and rubbed him with the ball down to his shoulders. Finally we placed the ball on his back and slowly rolled it up his neck and over his ears. Within 20 minutes of working with him we were able to roll the ball down his head and place a tarp over his head and neck without any problem. His fear of objects above his head had been solved.

Reagan takes Quinn for a ride

Quinn had been volunteering at the ranch for several months before Reagan arrived assisting with grooming and feeding some of the horses. When she saw Reagan for the first time her first question was can you ride him? Quinn and Reagan have become best friends and whenever she comes out to the ranch someone gets special treatment. Quinn takes him into the round pen and gives him a bowl of his senior grain mix and grooms him while he eats. She will carry on a conversation with Reagan telling him what a nice boy he is and what they are going to do that day. During the past two years they have really developed a relationship and Reagan now loves to go for lazy rides or walk along the fence line to eat grass with Quinn by his side. By interacting with Reagan two to three times a week,

Quinn has really helped him to become a very social horse when we ask him to interact with people. Between Quinn's visits I started to do some groundwork with Reagan asking him to respond to voice and hand signals, something he would pick up very quickly.

Reagan started to interact with Maddie and within a few days he would be following her around the ranch. It was as if she was trying to pass on some of her knowledge about the ranch to him. They were walking around the ranch together one day and we learned another lesson on how horses interact with each other. Maddie had learned to open the milk house door and another gate by using her mouth and if she thought a gate or door wasn't shut she would push against it with her nose. Maddie had just nickered to Reagan and she started to walk towards the milk house door. A few seconds later Reagan started to follow her until he was standing next to her by the door. Maddie grabbed the door handle with her lips and started to turn it several times until she finally opened it. I had been watching from a few yards away so I called out her name and said no as I closed the door. As I walked away I could hear the door handle moving again and having played this game so many times before I knew Maddie was back at the door. But to my surprise it was not Maddie opening the door. Reagan had walked up to the door and was now trying to open it with his lips. After several attempts he managed to open the door latch.

During the next few days Maddie and Reagan would walk up to that darn door and try to open it. Maddie had passed one of her trick on to another horse in the herd and Reagan now tries to open the door as she did.

Within a few months Reagan was ready to begin his new journey interacting with children and he quickly showed us what a good horse he was when a young girl visited the ranch.

Megan's Story

We recently received a phone call from a friend, whom we have know for many years, and she needed our help. Her granddaughter was visiting from Minnesota and she had a fear of animals caused by an incident when she was a toddler. Megan, now 12 years old, was strapped into a high chair when a dog came up underneath the high chair tray and starting nipping at her legs. Ever since that experience she had been afraid of animals in general and wouldn't let any animals approach her. Occasionally, Megan would try to approach dogs in her neighborhood very tentatively to pet them; more often she would avoid them. Knowing her grandchildren wanted to ride horses, she asked us if we could help a child overcome her fear of animals.

When Megan arrived at the ranch with her family, she walked behind her parents using them as a shield as they approached our gate. Some of the horses had walked up to the gate to greet our visitors and as we introduced them to some of the horses I noticed a very nervous young girl standing in the middle of the group. Walking from the gate to our round pen, someone was keeping a very watchful eye out for the horses and most likely thinking this wasn't going to be a good experience again. We entered our round pen to meet a thirty seven year old Quarter horse named Penny. Explaining how we greet and interact with our horses I demonstrated the horse handshake holding my arm towards the horse's nose and closing my hand into a fist I let the horses smell my hand. Megan's sisters and cousins eagerly greeted Penny and took turns brushing her. Megan wasn't quite ready to try it. We asked if she wanted to help hold the lead rope with us as I stood between Megan and Penny and she wanted to do that. After a few moments, she gave me the lead rope and slowly brushed Penny a few times. We introduced

Brie to everyone and as she was eating her grain we asked Megan to stand by us and slowly touch Brie's shoulder to feel how soft she felt. With some hesitation Megan slowly touched her shoulder. Then we asked if she wanted to touch the softest part of a horse, Brie's nose. Slowly her hand reached out to touch Brie's nose and we saw someone smile. We saddled Brie and after everyone had a chance to ride her, we asked Megan if she wanted to ride and her answer was yes. Megan cautiously put her foot into the stirrup and very slowly pulled herself into the saddle. Megan's legs were very stiff. We asked her to just relax and let her legs hang down the side of the saddle like a couple of noodles. Her response was a big smile. Slowly, Megan relaxed her legs and she could hold her arms in the air as Brie took a few steps and her smile got bigger.

Then Reagan was saddled for everyone to ride and Megan was more relaxed and smiling as she went for a ride. Megan was having so much fun that she rode Reagan with three other girls at the same time. Everyone was laughing and smiling including Megan. Reagan is an American Warm Blood and stands nearly sixteen hands high.

Finally Megan met Slice and we asked her if she ever wanted to be a cowgirl. She quickly replied yes. So she became a cowgirl by riding a cow named Slice as she was smiling and laughing. Today a young girl touched, brushed and rode a horse for the first time and she let the horses approach her and she greeted them with the horse handshake. As Megan and her family walked to the gate to leave, several horses walked next to them and a certain young girl was smiling.

In a little less than two hours a family learned how they could interact with horses and through a horse's gift of unconditional love, Megan had learned to overcome her fear of animals.

We called Megan's grandmother a few days later and asked if we could surprise Megan with a visitor before they headed home to Minnesota. She thought it was a great idea so Sue and I took a little road trip into town with Brie. We parked around the corner from their house and unloaded Brie from the trailer and put her saddle on. Walking up to their house on the sidewalk, some of the neighbors were probably wondering what the heck we were doing with a horse following us. Stopping on the front lawn, Brie started to munch on the grass and we could hear the sound of some excited voices inside the house. Suddenly Megan ran out the door and without any hesitation climbed right up in the saddle rubbing Brie's neck.

After everyone had another chance to go for a ride on Brie we asked Megan if she wanted to have her picture taken with her and she said yes. She thought she would sit in the saddle for the picture, but we had something else in mind. I crawled underneath Brie and asked Megan to join me for the photo. Without the slightest hesitation she crawled under Brie and smiled.

Helping one child or horse may not make a difference in the world, but it will make a world of difference to the one child or horse.

Megan is now babysitting for a family and they have a dog.

The Three Amigos

Several years ago someone that lived a few miles from us and attended the same church we did, mentioned to us one Sunday after church that her husband was going to an exotic animal sale with a friend. She was unsure of what he might bring home this time. A few weeks later, her husband stopped by the ranch and asked me where I bought our pony saddles and other tack equipment. He mentioned he had bought some ponies and a few other animals at a recent sale. I told him there was a local tack shop about twenty minutes away that could help him or there was a farm supply store nearby that also handled equine supplies. He had purchased the ponies for their grandchildren to enjoy. I occasionally saw them drive by the ranch and one day he stopped with two of his grandchildren to see our horses. When they got out of the car I could sense they were not really interested in looking at the horses. I asked how they liked the animals their grandfather had bought for them when they visited his house and didn't get a very enthusiastic reply. I thought to myself that grandpa enjoyed the animals more than the grandkids did. As it would turn out my intuition was right.

One day a car pulled up to the ranch and as I was walking over to see who it was, I could see the grandfather getting out of the car. He started to explain that the grandchildren had lost all interest in the animals and didn't even go out to the barn to see them anymore. After a couple of visits they had basically lost any interest they had. He had kept the animals for a couple of years thinking they might show an interest when they were older. But that was not the case. He was able to sell most of the smaller animals but was left with the three ponies, a mother and her daughter and another pony mare. He asked if we would be interested in looking at the ponies and he also had a couple of hundred bales of hay we could have. It was only about a five minute drive to their house so I said I would drive over to look at them. The mother and daughter were both little paints; the mother had black markings and the daughter brown markings and they both had very thick manes. The other mare was a bay color with a white blaze and also had a very thick mane. Their names were Annie, Stormy and Ginger. Annie was the mother of Stormy and supposedly could be ridden. Stormy was green, broke at best and very stand-offish. Ginger was not much better, but would let you approach her slowly and you could put a halter on her. Annie could be haltered and would walk with you on a lead rope. Stormy was a challenge, but she followed her mother everywhere walking right behind her. Once we able to catch them and put halters on them Annie and Ginger were fairly friendly. Stormy would pull against the lead rope for a few minutes, but then she settled down and you could rub on her neck and side. I was able to pick up their feet and they stood fairly still. They had all their vaccinations and they were using the same vet that we had. I made several trips hauling the hay home and then went to pick up the ponies. We opened up the trailer door and rather than trying to catch everyone it was easier to just let them explore the trailer and with a little encouragement they jumped right in. Upon arriving back at the ranch they whinnied to the other horses as they waited for me to open the door. I entered the trailer to put halters and lead ropes on them and they stood fairly still for me as I put a halter on Annie and Ginger. Stormy was leaning against Annie so I was able to reach over Annie's neck to slip a halter on Stormy. Once the trailer door was swung open they walked right out with me leading them. As I lead them into the pasture and took their lead ropes they quickly ran away exploring their new home.

The Three Amigos: Annie, Stormy and Ginger

I let them explore their new home for about half an hour and went out to the pasture to see if they would walk up to me for a treat. Annie was the leader of the group with Ginger running near her side and Stormy right behind her mother. After a few passes getting closer each time, I was able to turn away from them and start walking away and they slowly started to walk behind me getting closer and closer. Each time I would turn around to face them Stormy would backup and run in a big circle while Annie and Ginger walked in a little tighter circle around me. After a few more attempts to have them walk with me Annie was walking right behind me and I could turn around and rub her neck and shoulder. Ginger would slowly walk up to me and Stormy was still several feet away. Within a few days I was fairly confident that Stormy would catch on. What horse doesn't like horse treats?

Always running in the pasture together and eating right next to each other was how they got their nickname of the "three amigos". During the night if they lie down for awhile to sleep they are right on top of each other. When one walks into the barn to get a drink the others walk along or keep the others in sight to see where they are going. They are never more than a few yards from each other 24 hours a day.

The three amigos interact with the other horses in the herd. They will groom several of the other horses and run and play with the herd, but they maintain their own individual identity. Only Chocolate Chip, a POA gelding, has made any attempt to join their group. Maybe it's a boy thing that they will walk around with Chip, now the three girls keep him within eye sight.

Fortunately we were able to assist in this situation. This is probably the number one reason we hear when talking to individuals that call us wondering what to do with their horse. We bought a horse and now what do we do with it? The interest is lost and the parents are stuck dealing with a situation they easily could have avoided. If someone is interested in horses, find somewhere you can go and be around horses for awhile before rushing into purchasing one. Maybe someone you work with has a horse you could visit. Perhaps there is a riding stable in the area or possibly lease a horse for a summer to see how long the interest lasts.

A couple of years ago the grandfather pulled into our driveway and asked if the three horses were still here. He had the grandchildren with him and he thought they would like to see the horses again. We invited them in and a couple of our volunteers helped bring the three amigos out for the grandchildren to see. Now in their early teens, they had no interest in seeing the ponies again. The grandfather walked over to rub each of them on their neck; no one else wanted to touch them. Then there was a ringing sound. The horses had been replaced by cell phones.

The Canadian Kids

Legacy enjoys a carrot from Ashley

In 2006 and 2007 we purchased two horses from a Premarin Ranch in Manitoba, Canada. There has been so much already written about Premarin, and its part within the medical industry, that I am just going to briefly talk about it and then concentrate on the "kids." One of the ways the medical drug Premarin is manufactured is by the collection of the estrogen-enriched urine from the pregnant mares and thus the name pregnant mare urine (pre-mar-in). The mare's urine is captured in collection containers for the purpose of making this drug.

Once the foals have been weaned in August, the shipping of the foals usually began in late September and continued through November. The last week in September 2006, our first two babies arrived around 9:30 in the morning. They shared the 1,100 mile journey with thirteen other horses on their way for delivery throughout the U.S. When the trailer door slid open, we were lucky to see two little foals, with the tag numbers on their halters, right in front of us. After the driver had backed the trailer up to a small pen we had made with our horse panels, he entered the trailer to put lead ropes on the foals and they jumped out like they were shot out of cannons. We inspected them for any signs of injuries, signed the paperwork and within twenty minutes the driver was heading off to Illinois.

Legacy

After spending weeks looking at their photos online, and the long process of deciding which two we wanted, the next task was to think of names. The process of elimination was a long one to say the least. And of course once the names were picked, which one would get each name we had decided on? The little colt that came out of the trailer first would be named Legacy and the little gorgeous mare that followed would be named Destinee. Legacy is a buckskin color with a black mane and tail with strains of white in it. His mother is a black Quarter horse/Clydesdale cross and his father is a Palomino Quarter horse. Today, "Legs" as we affectionately call him is beautiful golden and tan colored Buckskin that is learning to respond to voice and hand signals.

Destinee's mother is a thoroughbred Percheron/Quarter horse cross and her father is a Palomino Quarter horse. A beautiful bay color with a black mane and tail with long eye lashes, Destinee is quite the looker. Everyone that visits the ranch thinks she is just drop dead gorgeous and she has a wonderful personality. She loves to chatter when she is around people for attention.

When the horses arrived at the ranch, they were four and a half months old. Within fifteen minutes of their arrival, we were able to walk them slowly to our round pen as they explored their new surroundings. Now they run to and from the pasture with the speed of the wind, love to roll in the fresh mud after a recent rain and anxiously greet us at the gate when we call their names.

Destinee

In 2007, we purchased two more foals from the same ranch in Canada and they arrived the third week of November. They were in a trail with sixteen other horses and had a very rough ride. The inspection station located at the Canadian and United States border made the hauler unload all of the horses from the trailer after waiting in one of the inspection lines for trucks for over three hours. So the 1,100 mile journey for the horses had three additional hours added on to their travel schedule. The hauler called us around 10:30 at night and said he was stopping in Minnesota to get a few hours of sleep and would get to the ranch around 10:00 a.m. the following morning. When I arrived home the next morning from work around 9:30 a.m., a large tractor trailer was just finishing backing into our driveway. We signed all of the paper work and then we opened up one of the side windows to look at the horses. There were eighteen horses in the trailer and the only way to separate the two we were getting was to unload all eighteen horses into our round pen. After unloading the horses from the trailer, we were able to divide the group of horses into two groups and helped the hauler reload the group that our two foals were not a part of. After sorting the remaining horses, we able to get our two foals to exit into another pen without any problems. As the final foals were reloaded the hauler asked for directions to a town about one hundred miles south of us; then he had deliveries in Indiana, Tennessee and Pennsylvania before heading to the east coast.

Amber shares a special moment with Destinee

We had decided on the two foals we were interested in fairly quickly and, when the ranch in Canada confirmed they were available, we reserved them right away. But we had not decided on any names and thought we would wait until we saw them in person to name them. The tiny foal that was black and white paint was easy to name – Oreo. The other foal, which appeared to be twice the size of Oreo, was named Nickers for the two white markings on her hind legs. Nickers and Oreo hadn't been handled as much as Legacy and Destinee when they were in Canada and it showed. Nickers bounced around like a rodeo horse and Oreo was quick to turn her rear end towards you. After spending about a half hour in the pen with them, I was able to clip a lead rope on their halters while they ate some of the hay I had given them. Getting them to walk the one hundred feet from the round pen into their box stall in the pole building was a little more challenging. I think we took three steps backwards for every one we took forward, but we eventually made it into their stalls. Oreo's mother is a grey thoroughbred/Percheron/Quarter horse cross and her father is the same as Legacy and Destinee's – a Palomino Quarter horse. Nickers' mother is a Percheron/Belgian cross and her father is a registered Paint. Oreo is a very lovely little girl and loves attention and mud. After it rains or after a fresh snowfall, she is the first one to roll. Nickers is turning into a big ham and has learned to love attention. She loves to have her ears and neck scratched; when you stop she will follow you around until you notice her again.

Oreo

Nickers

Saying 'Goodbye' to an Old Friend

When the holiday season comes and goes and the shock of what you spent on that "had to have it" present that's now collecting dust settles in, what's next? What about that New Year's resolution everyone makes? Ah, there is always next year. Some people spoil their pets and treat them like family; others think a pet is like a four-wheeler parked in the garage. Everyone wants that new toy or pet. The story we often tell is everyone wants the front end of horse or pet, but no one wants the back end.

When horses are young they're great to brush, bathe and ride for hours on end. As they get older, they're great to share treats with and maybe take short rides. When they enter their twilight years, they're great to push your face into and enjoy that "horse smell" and maybe just sit on their backs as they lazily walk around the pasture. Horses are herd animals and enjoy the company of each other and interacting with humans.

As an animal crazy child growing up in the city, I couldn't wait for Saturday mornings to come. I'd get up early, do my assigned household tasks and then wait for a hint from my mother that we were going to Herbbie and Berthas.

I'd grab my bottle of blue allergy pills, give them to my mom and reach for a glass of water. Sixty minutes later, as we arrived at my favorite to go with my parents, I raced into the house to take another allergy pill. Then I would run to the barn, while calling for their dog, Mugs. Herbbie raised trotting horses and one day he brought home a Shetland pony named Ginger for me. I'd climb over the fence and wait for him to whistle his special way calling the horses from the pasture. As Ginger ran into the barnyard, I'd have a halter on her before she could come to a stop. The rest of the day was spent riding bareback and brushing her as she ate grass. Before we headed home, I'd sneak some sugar cubes from Bertha's cupboard to give to Ginger. Years later Bertha would tell me she always had an extra box for me. Between the ages of nine and twelve, many weekends were spent with one of my best friends, Ginger.

Ginger

Forty years had past and I often think of the great times a city kid had with a horse. We were looking for a pony that we could use in our animal assisted therapy activities when a friend suggested we look at some of his ponies. As we pulled into his farm a pony caught my eye as she came up the gate. A smile came to my face as it did 40 years earlier. No she wasn't the same Ginger, but she had the buckskin markings and looked like someone I had known years ago.

Many things have changed over the years, but for the past fourteen years I could whistle or call her name and our Ginger would be at the gate waiting for us, nickering for her treats. Then one night Ginger didn't come to greet us.

Sue called out Ginger's name and she heard a faint nickering reply. Ginger was lying down in the barn. We were able to get her up and help her walk into a box stall and she laid down. After a while she was able to get up and eat, but then she laid down again. As we sat with Ginger, many of the other horses came over to the box stall, some making a strange low nicker sound and Ginger would softly replied to them. Chip, her best friend of over 25 years stood alone in the far corner of the barn. When the vet came into the stall, he slowly walked over to where he could see Ginger and softly nickered to her. Ginger slowly opened her eyes and looking at him, she nickered faintly in reply and then closed her eyes.

We could see it in her eyes and knew it in our hearts it was time for her to cross the Rainbow Bridge to reunite with those who had made the journey before her. As we sat with her throughout the night, Sue and I exchanged our favorite stories about Ginger. We had called our vet when we found Ginger that night and she arrived early the next morning. After listening to Ginger's heart, she told us her heart valves were worn out. As Sue held her head and rubbed her neck, Ginger was put to sleep and she began her new journey.

Ginger had given many children the joy of riding on a pony and for many of the children it was their first ride or first time they touched a horse. Many a child would grab a tuff of mane or bounce in the saddle, but Ginger always loved children and was never bothered. She was one of the first horses we used in our animal assisted therapy activities, visiting schools, nursing homes and senior citizen centers.

Our pets often give us expressions with their body language and their eyes. For Ginger it was sharing her gift of unconditional love with children. She always had that glow in her eyes when she was around children. Now, her eyes had showed us it was time for her to begin a new journey. Many of us have heard about or read the story of Crossing Over the Rainbow Bridge. As Ginger began to cross the bridge she could begin to see Woody, Peanut, Chynna and the others who passed before her waiting in a lush field of grass. Upon reaching the other side, she looked back at us and we could see the glow once again in her eyes and we knew that she would be waiting for us....

The 3 Cs & 3 Ts

Communication, commitment and consistency have become lost arts in today's fast paced society. And we have seen some pretty funny examples of what happens when individuals don't take the time to find the time to have the time.

We participated in a four day clinic held by an international equine clinician a few years ago. The first day was basic ground work and then we were in the saddle the following three days. An individual with a beautiful horse was having trouble controlling the horse right from the start and each day it continued to go downhill, but never asked for any assistance. The clinician had stated that if anyone had any questions or wanted him to work with them or ride your horse all you had to was just ask. We had asked him to ride our horse several times during the clinic. At the beginning of the fourth day we were riding in the round pen with several other participants and everyone knew the wreck was coming. The horse dropped his head and tossed the person over his neck and sent them rolling in the sand. The person sat up and shouted, "Now will you ride my damn horse?" The clinician said, "Sure. All you had to do was ask." The horse responded perfectly to the clinician's requests. Afterwards the person grabbed the reins and stormed out of the arena, shoved the horse in the trailer and sped off.

During an equine event that we were volunteering at, parents were following their child in a golf cart as she was riding her horse. The youth was dressed in full English attire for a demonstration. It had rained the night before and there was standing water in the ditches and puddles of water in the parking lots and drive lanes. As they approached a driveway with a ditch on both sides of it, the horse became nervous and was unsure of the water on the driveway. The parents pulled up behind the horse and bumped it in the hind legs with the golf cart trying to force it to go forward. The horse turned to the side and reared up on its hind legs and dumped the girl into the ditch filled with knee high water. We helped catch their horse and asked the girl if she was ok as she climbed out of the ditch soaked like a drowned rat. She grabbed the horse saying a few not so nice words to her parents and walked back to their trailer.

A parent was interested in volunteering at the ranch and had a child that was an experienced rider. They came out one day and after spending some time meeting the horses, I asked if their child would like to ride Maddie for a few minutes. I called Maddie and threw my saddle on her and helped the youth up into the saddle. Maddie walked right into the fence and stopped. I helped turn her away from the fence and she just turned and walked towards it again. The youth had no clue how to turn a horse left or right and Maddie knew she could do what ever she wanted. The parent said there must be something wrong with the horse and the youth thought she needed some more training. I asked Maddie to walk with me and we did several circles as I used hand and voice signals. The youth had gone trail riding out west on a trail horse that followed the horse ahead of it all day long.

Sue and I try to imitate the horses as much as we can when we interact with them. We'll walk in the pasture with them and kick the dirt, sit in a chair to see who is curious, walk quickly towards them and then suddenly turn away to see who might follow us. When we bringing them into the round pen, work with them in the round pen or what ever it may be we always must try to do three things. We must be consistent every time we interact with them, be committed to the task at hand and communicate with the horses in a manner that they will understand. Things are confusing enough for horses as we ask them to function in our world. The easier we make things for our horses, the easier they help make things for us.

If we never take the time to find the time, we'll never have the time to interact with our horses. We spend a few minutes each day touching every horse during the morning as we feed the horses and again during the evening feeding. As we call out their names we might ask them how their day was today, would they like a little treat or how the heck did they get so muddy after it rained. Each horse knows their name and most of the time will walk over to us when we ask them to and of course having some treats helps at times. The soft nudges and gentle nickers as we interact with the horses each day is something Sue and I can always find time for.

Our Animal Assisted Therapy Activities

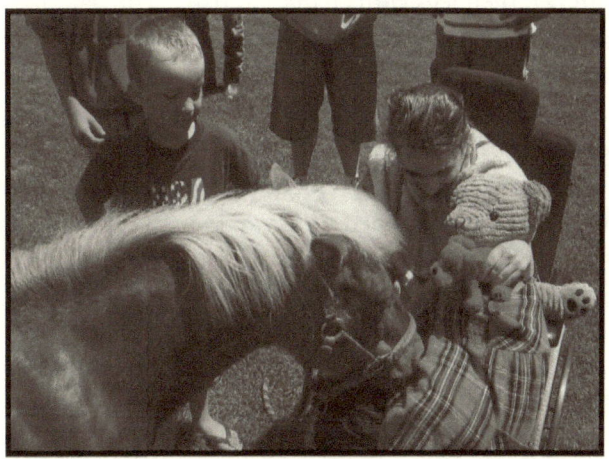

*Our "Thundering Herd" enjoy spending time
doing therapy within the community*

Throughout the years we have had the joy of seeing the benefits of using animals to help individuals with special needs. Our horses and other animals have visited children in early childhood exceptional needs programs and children with special needs in elementary and middle schools. The horses would help individuals improve their fine and cross motor skills, speech, self esteem and socialization skills through their interactions with the children. Although we did use other animals in our therapy programs, the horses were the most popular when we visited the schools.

The first thing necessary was selecting horses that had the personality to withstand being pushed, pulled, accidentally bumped by a wheelchair or have objects thrown at them to mention a few. We are blessed to have horses that even though they may have had hardships in their life, they all were great horses when interacting with individuals with special needs. Maddie, Brie, Peter, Patches, Reagan and Rusty were real troopers and on some days I wondered how they put up with some of the things that happened to them. We spent countless hours working with the horses getting them used to a variety of different situations. We walked across plastic tarps, through standing water, bounced rubber balls against their legs and body, bumped their legs with chairs and banged on pails to simulate different noises they would hear at a school. Grabbing a tuff of mane and holding their tail was also part of the process. So by the time we visited a school, we were confident the horses could handle whatever might come up. And they always did.

Maddie would have children crawling underneath her legs and she would never move an inch. Brie would have her mane pulled so hard it would take three adults to pry the child's hands loose. Patches was introduced to wet diapers. Rusty had a ball from a nearby kickball game bounce off his rump and Peter met a motorized wheelchair.

A boy was pouting and sitting in his chair. When one of the teacher aides would ask him a question, he wouldn't answer or made a grumpy reply. When Rusty came to visit the other children in the class, they couldn't wait to go outside and greet him. The boy was the only one left in the classroom, sitting in his chair refusing to get up. We went in and asked him if he wanted to go for a pony cart ride with Rusty and the reply was a slowly spoken yes. He got up out of his chair and walked outside to join the others, but he wanted to sit on the ground. So we suggested that he should go for a ride instead. He walked over to the pony cart and struggled to grasp the cart with his hand and lift his legs into the cart, but with a little assistance he did it. After the ride we asked him to pretend he was a cowboy and suddenly he slapped his side and galloped around the lawn area becoming very animated and vocal shouting, "Giddy-up! Giddy-up, Rusty!"

This child was moderately cognitive disabled and needed a brace to help support one of his legs; he was also visually impaired and limited to how much he could use his arms and hands. When the horses visited his class, he was always willing to brush a horse or share a carrot with them. It would take him a few moments to concentrate on grasping the lead rope or brush, but he was always willing to try. And when it's time to leave, he always gives us a high-five!

An early childhood exceptional needs child who has difficulty with speaking words or using them in a sentence was riding one of the ponies. Suddenly one of the teacher aides started calling out loud, "Did you hear that?" and began crying. One of the teachers suddenly had tears in her eyes. The child said the horse was "bumpy, bumpy" and smiled. It was the first time the child had said two words together without hesitating between them.

The class bully suddenly asked the child next to him if he would like to share the brush he had to help groom the pony. Earlier in the day, the little boy was given a time-out because he pushed someone down and took their toy.

A parent had written in her child's class journal that she had to rush off to pick up their other child from another school and without thinking put their cat in the car with their special needs son. The child would hit and push at their pets at home if he was left unattended. Suddenly she realized what she had done and when she looked into the rear view mirror in the car, she saw her son gently petting the cat. That night while sitting on the couch, she noticed he was holding the cat in his lap softly petting it. She thanked us for helping her son learn to be nice and gentle to animals. When we first met him, he would try to slap and hit the horses. We firmly held his hand and asked him to pet nicely. A few months later, he would calmly pet the horse's neck and shoulder.

We also visit nursing homes and senior citizen centers with the horses. The individuals will tell stories of growing up with horses on the farm or tell stories that their parents and grandparents had told them about using horse to work the fields, going to the store or riding a horse to school. The horses bring smiles to individuals as they retell their stories of years gone by.

Happy Tails

Sue and I hope you enjoyed reading the stories of the horses at Special Needs Ranch. I don't pretend to be an author or writer by any means, but instead someone who has been asked many times to share the horse's stories. There was a difficult time in our lives when Sue and I were both unemployed for a period of time and the bills were piling up faster than horse poop and we had to make a very tough decision. Should we save our house by selling the horses and other animals or should we keep what we truly believe we were meant to do. With very little hesitation we decided we needed to continue to provide the opportunity for horses to have a second chance in their life. At times it has been a rough journey and we have eaten Mac and Cheese on several occasions so we could provide the extra supplements, the special surgery for Trigger or to get through that long winter of high feed costs. But throughout the past sixteen years a few things have remained constant - the love that Sue and I share, as well as our commitment to making a difference in the lives of horses that have been abused, neglected, abandoned or are in need of assistance from an unforeseen situation.

A gentle nudge on the shoulder while awaiting their favorite treat, being greeted by the sound of a soft nicker as we approach the gate or kissing them one last time on their nose as they begin a new journey across the Rainbow Bridge, our lives have been enriched by horses. And we hope we have enriched the lives of others through their interactions with the horses.

Sue and I believe it is our calling to provide for horses in need and although we can't provide for every call for assistance, we give the horses that do arrive at the ranch the best opportunity we can for them to live their lives not in fear of abuse, but to interact as the herd animal God intended. Horses that have been mistreated will never forget, but they can learn to forgive and we are blessed to have the opportunity to provide a home for horses to have a second chance in their lives to share their unique gift of unconditional love with no questions asked.

God Bless and Happy Tails

www.ingramcontent.com/pod-product-compliance
Lightning Source LLC
Chambersburg PA
CBHW030346290526
45785CB00004B/1614